TEXTBOOK OF SUGAR CHEMISTRY

TEXTBOOK OF SUGAR CHEMISTRY

By

Amit Arora

DISCOVERY PUBLISHING HOUSE PVT. LTD.
NEW DELHI-110 002

Published by:
Tilak Wasan
DISCOVERY PUBLISHING HOUSE PVT. LTD.
4831/24, Ansari Road, Prahlad Street
Darya Ganj, New Delhi-110002 (India)
Phone: +91-11-23279245, 43764432
Fax: +91-11-23253475
E-mail: parul.wasan@gmail.com
discoverypublishinghouse@gmail.com
info@discoverypublishinggroup.com
web: www.discoverypublishinggroup.com

First Edition: 2011
ISBN: 978-81-8356-851-7

Textbook of Sugar Chemistry

Printed at:
Shree Balaji Art Press
Delhi

Preface

Sugar is a class of edible crystalline substances, mainly sucrose, lactose, and fructose. Human taste buds interpret its flavor as sweet. Sugar as a basic food carbohydrate primarily comes from sugar cane and from sugar beet, but also appears in fruit, honey, sorghum, sugar maple (in maple syrup), and in many other sources. It forms the main ingredient in much candy. Excessive consumption of sugar has been associated with increased incidences of type 2 diabetes, obesity and tooth decay.

Non-scientific use, the term sugar refers to sucrose (also called "table sugar" or "saccharose") a white crystalline solid disaccharide. In this informal sense, the word "sugar" principally refers to crystalline sugars.

Humans most commonly use sucrose as their sugar of choice for altering the flavor and properties (such as mouthful, preservation, and texture) of beverages and food. Commercially produced table sugar comes either from sugar cane or from sugar beet. Manufacturing and preparing food may involve other sugars, including palm sugar and fructose, generally obtained from corn (maize) or from fruit.

Sugar may dissolve in water to form a syrup. A great many foods exist which principally contain dissolved sugar. Generically known as "syrups", they may also have other more specific names such as "honey" or "molasses".

Scientifically, sugar refers to any monosaccharide or disaccharide. Monosaccharides (also called "simple sugars"), such as glucose, store chemical energy which biological cells convert to other types of energy.

In a list of ingredients, any word that ends with "-Glucose" (such as "glucose", "dextrose", "fructose", etc.) will likely denote a sugar. Sometimes such words may also refer to any types of carbohydrates soluble in water.

Glucose (a type of sugar found in human blood plasma) has the molecular formula $C_6 H_{12} O_6$.

In culinary terms, the foodstuff known as sugar delivers a primary taste sensation of sweetness. Apart from the many forms of sugar and of sugar-containing foodstuffs, alternative non-sugar-based sweeteners exist, and these particularly attract interest from people who have problems with their blood sugar level (such as diabetics) and people who wish to limit their calorie-intake while still enjoying sweet foods. Both natural and synthetic substitutes exist with no significant carbohydrate (and thus low-calorie) content: for instance stevia (a herb), and saccharin (produced from naturally occurring but not necessarily naturally edible substances by inducing appropriate chemical reactions).

Author

Contents

1 Introduction

Sugar is a class of edible crystalline substances, mainly sucrose, lactose, and fructose. Human taste buds interpret its flavor as sweet. Sugar as a basic food carbohydrate primarily comes from sugar cane and from sugar beet, but also appears in fruit, honey, sorghum, sugar maple (in maple syrup), and in many other sources. It forms the main ingredient in much candy. Excessive consumption of sugar has been associated with increased incidences of type 2 diabetes, obesity and tooth decay.

TERMINOLOGY

Popular

In non-scientific use, the term *sugar* refers to sucrose (also called "table sugar" or "saccharose"). Saccharose a white crystalline solid disaccharide. In this informal sense, the word "sugar" principally refers to crystalline sugars.

Humans most commonly use sucrose as their sugar of choice for altering the flavour and properties (such as mouthful, preservation, and texture) of beverages and food.

Commercially produced table sugar comes either from sugar cane or from sugar beet. Manufacturing and preparing food may involve other sugars, including palm sugar and fructose, generally obtained from corn (maize) or from fruit.

Sugar, granulated Nutritional value per 100 g (3.5 oz)	
Energy	390 kcal 1620 kJ
Carbohydrates	99.98 g
Sugars	99.91 g
Dietary fibre	0 g
Fat	0 g
Protein	0 g
Water	0.03 g
Riboflavin (Vit B_2)	0.019 mg (1%)
Calcium	1 mg (0%)
Iron	0.01 mg (0%)
Potassium	2 mg (0%)

Note: Percentages are relative to US recommendations for adults.

Source: USDA Nutrient database.

Sugar may dissolve in water to form a syrup. A great many foods exist which principally contain dissolved sugar. Generically known as "syrups", they may also have other more specific names such as "honey" or "molasses".

Scientific

Scientifically, *sugar* refers to any monosaccharide or disaccharide. Monosaccharides (also called "simple sugars"), such as glucose, store chemical energy which biological cells convert to other types of energy.

In a list of ingredients, any word that ends with "-ose" (such as "glucose", "dextrose", "fructose", etc.) will likely denote a sugar. Sometimes such words may also refer to any types of carbohydrates soluble in water.

Glucose (a type of sugar found in human blood plasma) has he molecular formula $C_6 H_{12} O_6$.

Culinary/Nutritional

In culinary terms, the foodstuff known as sugar delivers a primary taste sensation of sweetness. Apart from the many forms of sugar and of sugar-containing foodstuffs, alternative non-sugar-based sweeteners exist, and these particularly attract interest from people who have problems with their blood sugar level (such as diabetics) and people who wish to limit their calorie-intake while still enjoying sweet foods. Both natural and synthetic substitutes exist with no significant carbohydrate (and thus low-calorie) content: for instance stevia (a herb), and saccharin (produced from naturally occurring but not necessarily naturally edible substances by inducing appropriate chemical reactions).

History

Originally, people chewed the cane raw to extract its sweetness. Indians discovered how to crystallize sugar during the Gupta dynasty, around AD 350. Sugarcane was originally from tropical South Asia and Southeast Asia. Different species likely originated in different locations with *S. barberi* originating in India and *S. edule* and *S. officinarum* coming from New Guinea.

During the Muslim Agricultural Revolution, Arab entrepreneurs adopted the techniques of sugar production from India and then refined and transformed them into a large-scale industry. Arabs set up the first large scale sugar mills, refineries, factories and plantations.

The 1390s saw the development of a better press, which doubled the juice obtained from the cane. This permitted economic expansion of sugar plantations to Andalucia and to the Algarve. The 1420s saw sugar production extended to the Canary Islands, Madeira and the Azores.

The Portuguese took sugar to Brazil. Hans Staden, published in 1555, writes that by 1540 Santa Catarina Island had 800 sugar mills and that the north coast of Brazil, Demarara and Surinam had another 2,000. Approximately 3,000 small mills built before 1550 in the New World created an unprecedented demand for cast iron gears, levers, axles and other implements. Specialist trades in mold-making and iron-casting developed in Europe due to the expansion of sugar production. Sugar mill construction developed technological skills needed for a nascent industrial revolution in the early 17th century.

After 1625 the Dutch carried sugarcane from South America to the Caribbean islands — where it became grown from Barbados to the Virgin Islands. The years 1625 to 1750 saw sugar become worth its weight in gold. With the European colonization of the Americas, the Caribbean became the world's largest source of sugar. These islands could supply sugarcane using slave labor and produce sugar at prices vastly lower than those of cane sugar imported from the East.

During the eighteenth century, sugar became enormously popular and the sugar market went through a series of booms. As Europeans established sugar plantations on the larger Caribbean islands, prices fell, especially in Britain. By the eighteenth century all levels of society had become common consumers of the former luxury product. At first most sugar in Britain went into tea, but later confectionery and chocolates became extremely popular. Suppliers commonly sold sugar in solid cones and consumers required a sugar nip, a pliers-like tool, to break off pieces.

Beginning in the late 18th century, the production of sugar became increasingly mechanized. The steam engine first powered a sugar mill in Jamaica in 1768, and soon after, steam replaced direct firing as the source of process heat. During the same century, Europeans began experimenting with sugar production from other crops. Andreas Marggraf identified sucrose in beet root and his student Franz Achard built a sugar beet processing factory in Silesia. However the beet-sugar industry really took off during the Napoleonic Wars, when France and the continent were cut off from caribbean sugar. Today 30% of the world's sugar is produced from beets.

Today, a large beet refinery producing around 1,500 tonnes of sugar a day needs a permanent workforce of about 150 for 24-hour production.

Etymology

In the case of sugar, the etymology reflects the spread of the commodity. The English word "sugar" originates from the Arabic and Persian word *sukkar*, itself derived from Sanskrit *Sharkara*. It came to English by way of French, Spanish and/or Italian, which derived their word for sugar from the Arabic and Persian *shakar* (whence the Portuguese word *açúcar*, the Spanish word *azúcar*, the Italian word *zucchero*, the Old French word *zuchre* and the contemporary French word *sucre*). The Greek word for "sugar", *Zàxapn zahari*, means "pebble". Note that the English word *jaggery* (meaning "coarse brown Indian sugar") has similar ultimate etymological origins (presumably in Sanskrit).

Refined sugar was originally a luxury, but sugar eventually became sufficiently cheap and common to influence standard cuisine. Britain and the Caribbean islands have cuisines where the use of sugar became particularly prominent.

Sugar forms a major element in confectionery and in desserts. Cooks use it as a food preservative as well as for sweetening.

Studies have indicated potential links between processed sugar consumption and health hazards, including obesity and tooth decay. John Yudkin showed that the consumption of sugar and refined sweeteners is closely associated with coronary heart disease. It is also considered as a source of endogenous glycation processes.

Tooth Decay

Tooth decay has arguably become the most prominent health hazard associated with the consumption of sugar. Oral bacteria such as *Streptococcus mutans* live in dental plaque and metabolize sugars into lactic acid. High concentrations of acid may result on the surface of a tooth, leading to tooth demineralization

Diabetes

Diabetes, a disease that causes the body to metabolize sugar poorly, occurs when either:

- the body attacks the cells producing insulin, the chemical that allows the metabolizing of sugar in the body's cells (Type 1 diabetes);
- the body's cells ignore insulin (Type 2 diabetes).

When glucose builds up in the bloodstream, it can cause two problems:

1. in the short term, cells become starved for energy because they do not have access to the glucose.
2. in the long term, frequent glucose build-up increases the acidity of the blood, damaging many of the body's organs, including the eyes, kidneys, nerves and/or heart.

Authorities advise diabetics to avoid sugar-rich foods to prevent adverse reactions.

Obesity

In the United States of America, a scientific/health debate has started over the causes of a steep rise in obesity in the general population — and one view posits increased consumption of carbohydrates in recent decades as a major factor.

Obesity can result from a number of factors including:

- an increased intake of energy-dense foods — high in fat and sugars but low in vitamins, minerals and other micronutrients; and
- decreased physical activity.

The National Health and Nutrition Examination Survey I indicates that the population in the United States has increased its proportion of energy consumption from carbohydrates and decreased its proportion from total fat while obesity has increased. This implies, along with the United Nations report cited below, that obesity may correlate better with sugar consumption than with fat consumption, and that reducing fat consumption while increasing sugar consumption actually increases the level of obesity. Table 1.1 summarizes this study (based on the proportion of energy intake from different food sources for US Adults 20-74 years old, as carried out by the U.S. Department of Health and Human Services, Centers for Disease Control and Prevention, National Center for Health Statistics, Hyattsville, MD.

Table 1.1

Year	Sex	Carbohydrate	Fat	Protein	Obesity
1971	Male	42.4%	36.9%	16.5%	12.1%
1971	Female	45.4%	36.1%	16.9%	16.6%
2000	Male	49.0%	32.8%	15.5%	27.7%
2000	Female	51.6%	32.8%	15.1%	34.0%

Another study published in 2002 and conducted by the National Academy of Sciences over a 3-year period concluded: "There is no clear and consistent association between increased intakes of added sugars and BMI." (BMI or "Body mass index" measures body-weight and height.)

Gout

Researchers have implicated sugary drinks high in fructose in a surge in cases of the painful joint disease gout.

Cancer

A link between sugar and cancer has been conjectured for some time but this remains a controversial topic. Some studies lend support to this theory. However no major medical or nutritional organization currently recommends reducing sugar consumption to prevent cancer.

United Nations Nutritional Advice

In 2003, four United Nations agencies, [including the World Health Organization (WHO) and the Food and Agriculture Organization (FAO)] commissioned a report compiled by a panel of 30 international experts. The panel stated that the total of free sugars (all monosaccharides and disaccharides added to foods by manufacturers, cooks or consumers, plus sugars naturally present in honey, syrups and fruit juices) should not account for more than 10% of the energy intake of a healthy diet, while carbohydrates in total should represent between 55% and 75% of the energy intake.

Debate on Extrinsic Sugar

Argument continues as to the value of extrinsic sugar (sugar added to food) compared to that of intrinsic sugar (naturally present in food). Adding sugar to food particularly enhances taste, but does increase the total number of calories, among other negative effects on health and physiology.

In the United States of America, sugar has become increasingly evident in food products, as more food manufacturers add sugar or high fructose corn syrup to a wide variety of consumables. Candy bars, soft drinks, chips, snacks, fruit juice, peanut butter, soups, ice cream, jams, jellies, yogurt, and many breads may have added sugars.

Concerns of Vegetarians and Vegans

The sugar refining industry often uses bone char (calcinated animal bones) for decolourizing This may concern some vegans and vegetarians; about a quarter of the sugar in the U.S. is processed using bone char as a filter and the rest is processed with activated carbon. As bone char does not get into the sugar, the relevant authorities consider sugar processed this way as parve/kosher.

Vegetarians and vegans may also object to the impact that the burning of the cane fields (a common part of the harvesting practice) has on insects, rats, snakes, and other life residing in the fields.

Production

Table sugar (sucrose) comes from plant sources. Two important sugar crops predominate: sugarcane (*Saccharum spp.*) and sugar beets (*Beta vulgaris*), in which sugar can account for 12% to 20% of the plant's dry weight. Some minor commercial sugar crops include the date palm (*Phoenix dactylifera*), sorghum (*Sorghum vulgare*), and the sugar maple (*Acer saccharum*). In the financial year 2001/2002, worldwide production of sugar amounted to 134.1 million tonnes.

The first production of sugar from sugarcane took place in India. Alexander the Great's companions reported seeing "honey produced without the intervention of bees" and it remained exotic in Europe until the Arabs started cultivating it in Sicily and Spain. Only after the Crusades did it begin to rival honey as a sweetener in Europe. The Spanish began cultivating sugarcane in the West Indies in 1506 (and in Cuba in 1523). The Portuguese first cultivated sugarcane in Brazil in 1532.

Most cane sugar comes from countries with warm climates, such as Brazil, India, China, Thailand, Mexico and Australia, the top sugar-producing countries in the world. Brazil overshadows most countries, with roughly 30 million tonnes of cane sugar produced in 2006, while India produced 21 million, China 11 million, and Thailand and Mexico roughly 5 million each. Viewed by region, Asia predominates in cane sugar production, with large contributions from China, India and Thailand and other countries combining to account for 40% of global production in 2006. South America comes in second place with 32% of global production; Africa and Central America each produce 8% and Australia 5%. The United States, the Caribbean and Europe make up the remainder, with roughly 3% each.

Beet sugar comes from regions with cooler climates: northwest and eastern Europe, northern Japan, plus some areas in the United States (including California). In the northern hemisphere, the beet-growing season ends with the start of harvesting around September. Harvesting and processing continues until March in some cases. The availability of processing plant capacity, and the weather both influence the duration of harvesting and processing - the industry can lay up harvested beet until processed, but a frost-damaged beet becomes effectively unprocessable.

The European Union (EU) has become the world's second-largest sugar exporter. The Common Agricultural Policy of the EU sets maximum quotas for members' production to match supply and demand, and a price. Europe exports excess production quota (approximately 5 million tonnes in 2003). Part of this, "quota" sugar, gets subsidised from industry levies, the remainder (approximately half) sells as "C quota" sugar at market prices without subsidy. These subsidies and a high import tariff make it difficult for other countries to export to the EU states, or to compete with the Europeans on world markets.

The United States sets high sugar prices to support its producers, with the effect that many former consumers of sugar have switched to corn syrup (beverage manufacturers) or moved out of the country (candymakers).

The cheap prices of glucose syrups produced from wheat and corn (maize) threaten the traditional sugar market. Used in combination with artificial sweeteners, they can allow drink manufacturers to produce very low-cost goods.

Cane

Since the 6th century BC cane sugar producers have crushed the harvested vegetable material from sugarcane in order to collect and filter the juice. They then treat the liquid (often with lime (calcium oxide)) to remove impurities and then neutralize it. Boiling the juice then allows the sediment to settle to the bottom for dredging out, while the scum rises to the surface for skimming off. In cooling, the liquid crystallizes, usually in the process of stirring, to produce sugar crystals. Centrifuges usually remove the uncrystallized syrup. The producers can then either sell the resultant sugar, as is, for use; or process it further to produce lighter grades. This processing may take place in another factory in another country. Sugar cane appears fourth in the list for agriculture in China.

Beet

Beet sugar producers slice the washed beets, then extract the sugar with hot water in a "diffuser". An alkaline solution ("milk of lime" and carbon dioxide from the lime kiln) then serves to precipitate impurities After filtration, evaporation concentrates the juice to a content of about 70% solids, and controlled crystallisation extracts the sugar. A centrifuge removes the sugar crystals from the liquid, which gets recycled in the crystalliser stages. When economic constraints prevent the removal of more sugar, the manufacturer discards the remaining liquid, now known as molasses.

Sieving the resultant white sugar produces different grades for selling.

Cane Versus Beet

Little perceptible difference exists between sugar produced from beet and that from cane. Chemical tests can distinguish the two, and some tests aim to detect fraudulent abuse of European Union subsidies or to aid in the detection of adulterated fruit juice.

The production of sugarcane needs approximately four times as much water as the production of sugar beet, therefore some countries that traditionally produced cane sugar (such as Egypt) have seen the building of new beet sugar factories recently. On the other hand, sugar cane tolerates hot climates better. Some sugar factories process both sugar cane and sugar beets and extend their processing period in that way.

The production of sugar results in residues which differ substantially depending on the raw materials used and on the place of production. While cooks often use cane molasses in food preparation, humans find molasses from sugar beet unpalatable, and it therefore ends up mostly as industrial fermentation feedstock (for example in alcohol distilleries), or as animal feed. Once dried, either type of molasses can serve as fuel for burning.

Culinary Sugars

So-called raw sugars comprise yellow to brown sugars made by clarifying the source syrup by boiling and drying with heat, until it becomes a crystalline solid, with minimal chemical processing. Raw beet sugars result from the processing of sugar beet juice, but only as intermediates *en route* to white sugar. Types of raw sugar include *demerara*, *muscovado*, and *turbinado*. Mauritius and Malawi export significant quantities of such specialty sugars. Manufacturers sometimes prepare raw sugar as loaves rather than as a crystalline powder, by pouring sugar and molasses together into molds and allowing the mixture to dry. This results in sugar-cakes or loaves, called *jaggery* or *gur* in India, *pingbian tang* in China, and *panela, panocha, pile, piloncillo* and *pão-de-açúcar* in various parts of Latin America. In South America, truly raw sugar, unheated and made from sugarcane grown on farms, does not have a large market-share.

Mill white sugar, also called plantation white, crystal sugar, or superior sugar, consists of raw sugar where the production process does not remove colored impurities, but rather bleaches them white by exposure to sulfur dioxide. Though the most common form of sugar in sugarcane-growing areas, this product does not store or ship well; after a few weeks, its impurities tend to promote discoloration and clumping.

Blanco directo, a white sugar common in India and other south Asian countries, comes from precipitating many impurities out of the cane juice by using *phosphatation* — a treatment with phosphoric acid and calcium hydroxide similar to the carbonatation technique used in beet sugar refining. In terms of sucrose purity, blanco directo is more pure than mill white, but less pure than white refined sugar.

White refined sugar has become the most common form of sugar in North America as well as in Europe. Refined sugar can be made by dissolving raw sugar and purifying it with a phosphoric acid method similar to that used for blanco directo, a carbonatation process involving calcium hydroxide and carbon dioxide, or by various filtration strategies. It is then further purified by filtration through a bed of activated carbon or bone char depending on where the processing takes place. Beet sugar refineries produce refined white sugar directly without an intermediate raw stage. White refined sugar is typically sold as *granulated sugar,* which has been dried to prevent clumping.

Granulated sugar comes in various crystal sizes — for home and industrial use — depending on the application:

- Coarse-grained sugars, such as *sanding sugar* (also called "pearl sugar", "decorating sugar", *nibbed sugar* or *sugar nibs*) adds "sparkle" and flavor for decorating to baked goods, candies, cookies/biscuits and other desserts. The sparkling effect occurs because the sugar forms large crystals which reflect light. Sanding sugar, a large-crystal sugar, serves for making edible decorations. It has larger granules that sparkle when sprinkled on baked goods and candies and will not dissolve when subjected to heat.
- Normal granulated sugars for table use: typically they have a grain size about 0.5 mm across.
- Finer grades result from selectively sieving the granulated sugar.
- *caster* (or *castor*·) (0.35 mm), commonly used in baking, originally sprinkled from a castor.
- *superfine* sugar, also called *baker's sugar*, *berry sugar*, or *bar sugar* — favored for sweetening drinks or for preparing meringue.
- Finest grades.
- *Powdered sugar*, *10X sugar*, *confectioner's sugar* (0.060 mm), or *icing sugar* (0.024 mm), produced by grinding sugar to a fine powder. The manufacturer may add a small amount of anticaking agent to prevent clumping — either cornstarch (1% to 3%) or tri-calcium phosphate.

Retailers also sell sugar cubes or lumps for convenient consumption of a standardized amount. Suppliers of sugarcubes make them by mixing sugar crystals with sugar syrup. Jakub Kryštof Rad invented sugarcubes in 1841 in the Austrian Empire (what is now the Czech Republic).

Brown sugars come from the late stages of sugar refining, when sugar forms fine crystals with significant molasses content, or from coating white refined sugar with a cane molasses syrup. Their color and taste become stronger with increasing molasses content, as do their moisture-retaining properties. Brown sugars also tend to harden if exposed to the atmosphere, although proper handling can reverse this.

The World Health Organisation and the Food and Agriculture Organization of the United Nations expert report (WHO Technical Report Series 916 Diet, Nutrition and the Prevention of Chronic Diseases) defines free sugars as all monosaccharides and disaccharides added to foods by the manufacturer, cook or consumer, plus sugars naturally present in honey, syrups and fruit juices. This includes all the sugars referred to above. The term distinguishes these forms from all other *culinary sugars* added in their natural form with no refining at all.

Natural sugars comprise all completely unrefined sugars: effectively all sugars not defined as *free sugars*. The WHO Technical Report Series 916 Diet, Nutrition and the Prevention of Chronic Diseases approves only natural sugars as carbohydrates for unrestricted consumption. Natural sugars come in fruit, grains and vegetables in their natural or cooked form.

Chemistry

Biochemists regard sugars as relatively simple carbohydrates. Sugars include monosaccharides, disaccharides, trisaccharides and the oligosaccharides - containing 1, 2, 3, and 4 or more monosaccharide units respectively. Sugars contain either aldehyde groups (-CHO) or ketone groups (C=O), where there are carbon-oxygen double bonds, making the sugars reactive. Most simple sugars (monosaccharides) conform to $(CH_2O)n$ where n is between 3 and 7. A notable exception, deoxyribose, as its name suggests, has a "missing" oxygen atom. All saccharides with more than one ring in their structure result from two or more monosaccharides joined by glycosidic bonds with the resultant loss of a molecule of water (H_2O) per bond. Sugars can also be used as monomers to create biopolymers such as cellulose, which is made of glucose, or DNA, which uses deoxyribose as a backbone.

As well as using classifications based on their reactive group, chemists may also subdivide sugars according to the number of carbons they contain. Derivatives of trioses ($C_3H_6O_3$) are intermediates in glycolysis. Pentoses (5-carbon sugars) include ribose and deoxyribose, which form part of nucleic acids. Ribose also forms a component of several chemicals that have importance in the metabolic process, including NADH and ATP. Hexoses (6-carbon sugars) include glucose, a universal substrate for the production of energy in the form of ATP. Through photosynthesis plants produce glucose, which has the formula $C_6H_{12}O_6$, and convert it for storage as an energy reserve in the form of other carbohydrates such as starch, or (as in cane and beet) as sucrose (table sugar). Sucrose has the chemical formula $C_{12}H_{22}O_{11}$.

Many pentoses and hexoses can form ring structures. In these closed-chain forms, the aldehyde or ketone group remains unfree, so many of the reactions typical of these groups cannot occur. Glucose in solution exists mostly in the ring form at equilibrium, with less than 0.1% of the molecules in the open-chain form.

Monosaccharides in a closed-chain form can form glycosidic bonds with other monosaccharides, creating disaccharides (such as sucrose) and polysaccharides (such as starch). Enzymes must hydrolyse or otherwise break these glycosidic bonds before such compounds become metabolised. After digestion and absorption, the principal monosaccharides present in the blood and internal tissues include glucose, fructose, and galactose.

The prefix "glyco-" indicates the presence of a sugar in an otherwise non-carbohydrate substance. Note for example glycoproteins, proteins connected to one or more sugars.

Monosaccharides include fructose, glucose, galactose and mannose. Disaccharides occur most commonly as sucrose (cane or beet sugar - made from one glucose and one fructose), lactose (milk sugar - made from one glucose and one galactose) and maltose (made of two glucoses). These disaccharides have the formula $C_{12}H_{22}O_{11}$.

Hydrolysis can convert sucrose into a syrup of fructose and glucose, producing *invert sugar*. This resulting syrup, sweeter than the original sucrose has uses in making confections because it does not crystallize as easily and thus produces a smoother finished product.

If combined with fine ash, sugar will burn with a blue flame.

Measuring Sugar

Scientists and the sugar industry use degrees Brix (symbol °Bx), introduced by Antoine Brix, as units of measurement of the mass ratio of dissolved substance to water in a liquid. A 25 °Bx sucrose solution has 25 grams of sucrose per 100 grams of liquid; or, to put it another way, 25 grams of sucrose sugar and 75 grams of water exist in the 100 grams of solution.

An infrared Brix sensor measures the vibrational frequency of the sugar molecules, giving a Brix degrees measurement. This does not equate to Brix degrees from a density or refractive index measurement because it will specifically measure dissolved sugar concentration instead of all dissolved solids. When using a refractometer, one should report the result as "refractometric dried substance" (RDS). One might speak of a liquid as having 20 °Bx RDS. This refers to a measure of percent by weight of *total* dried solids and, although not technically the same as Brix degrees determined through an infrared method, renders an accurate measurement of sucrose content, since sucrose in fact forms the majority of dried solids. The advent of in-line infrared

Brix measurement sensors has made measuring the amount of dissolved sugar in products economical using a direct measurement.

Purity

Technicians usually measure the purity (sucrose content) of sugar by polarimetry — the measurement of the rotation of plane-polarized light by a solution of sugar.

Baking Weight/Mass Volume Relationship

Different culinary sugars have different densities due to differences in particle size and inclusion of moisture.

The Domino Sugar Company has established the following volume to weight conversions:

- Brown sugar 1 cup = 195g = 6.88 oz
- Granular sugar 1 cup = 200g = 7.06 oz
- Powdered sugar 1 cup = 120g = 4.23 oz

Trade and Economics

Historically one of the most widely-traded commodities in the world, sugar accounts for around 2% of the global dry cargo market. International sugar prices show great volatility, ranging from around 3 to over 60 cents per pound in the past 50 years. Of the world's 180-odd countries, around 100 produce sugar from beet or cane, a few more refine raw sugar to produce white sugar, and all countries consume sugar. Consumption of sugar ranges from around 3 kilograms per person per annum in Ethiopia to around 40 kg/person/yr in Belgium. Consumption per capita rises with income per capita until it reaches a plateau of around 35 kg per person per year in middle income countries.

Many countries subsidize sugar production heavily. The European Union, the United States, Japan and many developing countries subsidize domestic production and maintain high tariffs on imports. Sugar prices in these countries have often exceeded prices on the international market by up to three times; today, with world market sugar futures prices currently strong, such prices typically exceed world prices by two times.

Within international trade bodies, especially in the World Trade Organization, the "G20" countries led by Brazil have long argued that because these sugar markets essentially exclude cane sugar imports, the G20 sugar producers receive lower prices than they would under free trade. While both the European Union and United States maintain trade agreements whereby certain developing and less developed country (LDCs) can sell certain quantities of sugar into their markets, free of the usual import tariffs, countries outside these preferred trade régimes have complained that these arrangements violate the "most favoured nation" principle of international trade. This has led to numerous tariffs and levies in the past.

In 2004, the WTO sided with a group of cane sugar exporting nations (led by Brazil and Australia) and ruled the EU sugar-régime and the accompanying ACP-EU Sugar Protocol (whereby a group of African, Caribbean, and Pacific countries receive preferential access to the European sugar market) illegal. In response to this and to other rulings of the WTO, and owing to internal pressures on the EU sugar-régime, the European Commission proposed on 22 June 2005 a radical reform of the EU sugar-régime, cutting prices by 39% and eliminating all EU sugar exports. The African, Caribbean, Pacific and least developed country sugar exporters reacted with dismay to the EU sugar proposals, On 25 November 2005 the Council of the EU agreed to cut EU sugar prices by 36% as from 2009. In 2007 it seemed that the U.S. Sugar Program could become the next target for reform. However, some commentators expected heavy lobbying from the U.S. sugar industry, which donated $2.7 million to US House and US Senate incumbents in the 2006

US election, more than any other group of US food-growers. Especially prominent lobbyists include The Fanjul Brothers, so-called "sugar barons" who made the single largest individual contributions of soft money to both the Democratic and Republican parties in the political system of the United States of America.

Small quantities of sugar, especially specialty grades of sugar, reach the market as 'fair trade' commodities; the fair trade system produces and sells these products with the understanding that a larger-than-usual fraction of the revenue will support small farmers in the developing world. However, whilst the Fairtrade Foundation offers a premium of USD 60.00 per tonne to small farmers for sugar branded as "Fairtrade" government schemes such the U.S. Sugar Program and the ACP Sugar Protocol offer premiums of around USD 400.00 per tonne above world market prices. However, the EU announced on 14 September 2007 that it had offered "to eliminate all duties and quotas on the import of sugar into the EU".

The Sugar Association has launched a campaign to promote sugar over artificial substitutes. The Association now aggressively challenges many common beliefs regarding negative side effects of sugar consumption. The campaign aired a high-profile television commercial during the 2007 Prime Time Emmy Awards on FOX Television. The Sugar Association uses the trademark tagline "Sugar: sweet by nature."

History of Sugar

The history of sugar reflects industrial growth . Most humans appreciate sweet tastes. This has created demand for sweeteners, which in turn has fueled increases in the production of sugar, making more sugar available at affordable prices (within the constraints of soil-fertility, land-availability and a supply of biddable labour), leading to the development of more food products containing sugar and the addition of more sugar to existing products, accompanied by a growing average intake of sugar by consumers.

Because of the need for labour-intensive processing to turn sugarcane into end-products, much of the history of the sugar industry has had associations with large-scale slavery.

Early Use of Sugarcane in India

Originally, people chewed sugarcane raw to extract its sweetness. Indians discovered how to crystallize sugar during the Gupta dynasty, around AD 350 Sugarcane was originally from tropical South Asia and Southeast Asia Different species likely originated in different locations with *S. barberi* originating in India and *S. edule* and *S. officinarum* coming from New Guinea.

However, sugar remained relatively unimportant until the Indians discovered methods of turning sugarcane juice into granulated crystals that were easier to store and to transport Crystallized sugar was discovered by the time of the Imperial Guptas. Indian sailors, consumers of clarified butter and sugar, carried sugar by various trade routes Travelling Buddhist monks brought sugar crystalization methods to China. During the reign of Harsha in North India, Indian envoys in Tang China taught sugarcane cultivation methods after Emperor Taizong of Tang made his interest in sugar known, and China soon established its first sugarcane cultivation in the seventh century Chinese documents confirm at least two missions to India, initiated in 647 CE, for obtaining technology for sugar-refining In South Asia, the Middle East and China, sugar became a staple of cooking and desserts.

Early refining methods involved grinding or pounding the cane in order to extract the juice, and then boiling down the juice or drying it in the sun to yield sugary solids that looked like gravel. The Sanskrit word for sugar '*sharkara*' also means "gravel" or "Sand". Similarly, the Chinese use the term "gravel sugar" for what the West knows as "table sugar".

Cane Sugar in the Muslim World and Europe

During the Muslim Agricultural Revolution, Arab entrepreneurs adopted sugar production techniques from India and then refined and transformed them into a large-scale industry. Arabs set up the first sugar mills, refineries, factories and plantations. The Arabs and Berbers spread the cultivation of sugar throughout the Arab Empire and across much of the Old World, including Western Europe after they conquered the Iberian Peninsula in the eighth century CE Ponting traces the spread of the cultivation of sugarcane from its introduction into Mesopotamia, then the Levant and the islands of the eastern Mediterranean, especially Cyprus, by the 10th century He also notes that it spread along the coast of East Africa to reach Zanzibar.

Crusaders brought sugar home with them to Europe after their campaigns in the Holy Land, where they encountered caravans carrying "sweet salt". Early in the 12th century, Venice acquired some villages near Tyre and set up estates to produce sugar for export to Europe, where it supplemented honey as the only other available sweetener Crusade chronicler William of Tyre, writing in the late 12th century, described sugar as "very necessary for the use and health of mankind".

Ponting recounts the trials of the early European sugar entrepreneurs.

The crucial problem with sugar production was that it was highly labour-intensive in both growing and processing. Because of the huge weight and bulk of the raw cane it was very costly to transport, especially by land, and therefore each estate had to have its own factory. There the cane had to be crushed to extract the juices, which were boiled to concentrate them, in a series of back-breaking and intensive operations lasting many hours. However, once it had been processed and concentrated the sugar had a very high value for its bulk and could be traded over long distances by ship at a considerable profit. The [European sugar] industry only began on a major scale after the loss of the Levant to a resurgent Islam and the shift of production to Cyprus under a mixture of Crusader aristocrats and Venetian merchants. The local population on Cyprus spent most of their time growing their own food and few would work on the sugar estates. The owners, therefore, brought in slaves from the Black Sea area (and a few from Africa) to do most of the work. The level of demand and production was low and therefore so was the trade in slaves—no more than about a thousand people a year. It was little greater when sugar production began in Sicily. In the Atlantic islands [the Canaries, Madeira, and the Cape Verde Islands], once the initial exploitation of the timber and raw materials was over, it rapidly became clear that sugar production would be the most profitable way of using the new territories. The problem was the heavy labour involved—the Europeans refused to work as more than supervisors. The solution was to bring in slaves from Africa. The crucial developments in this trade began in the 1440s.

The 1390s saw the development of a better press, which doubled the juice obtained from the cane. This permitted economic expansion of sugar plantations to Andalucia and to the Algarve. The 1420s saw sugar production extended to the Canary Islands. It started in Madeira in 1455, using advisers from Sicily and (largely) Genoese capital for the mills. The accessibility of Madeira attracted Genoese and Flemish traders keen to bypass Venetian monopolies. "By 1480 Antwerp had some seventy ships engaged in the Madeira sugar trade, with the refining and distribution concentrated in Antwerp. By the 1490s Madeira had overtaken Cyprus as a producer of sugar. African slaves also worked in the sugar plantations of the Kingdom of Castile around Valencia.

Sugar Cultivation in the New World

In August 1492 Christopher Columbus stopped at Gomera in the Canary Islands, for wine and water, intending to stay only four days. He became romantically involved with the Governor of the island, Beatrice de Bobadilla, and stayed a month. When he finally sailed she gave him cuttings of sugarcane, which became the first to reach the New World.

The Portuguese took sugar to Brazil. By 1540, Santa Catalina Island had 800 sugar mills and the north coast of Brazil, Demarara, and Surinam had another 2000. Hispaniola had its first sugar harvest in 1501. Sugar mills had been constructed in Cuba and Jamaica by the 1520s. Approximately 3000 small mills built before 1550 in the New World created an unprecedented demand for cast iron gears, levers, axles and other implements. Specialist trades in mold-making and iron-casting developed in Europe due to the expansion of sugar production. Sugar mill construction developed technological skills needed for a nascent industrial revolution in the early 17th century.

After 1625 the Dutch carried sugarcane from South America to the Caribbean islands, where it was grown from Barbados to the Virgin Islands. The years 1625 to 1750 saw sugar become worth its weight in gold Contemporaries often compared the worth of sugar with valuable commodities including musk, pearls, and spices. Prices declined slowly as production became multi-sourced, especially through British colonial policy. Formerly an indulgence of the rich, sugar became increasingly common among the poor. Sugar production increased in mainland North American colonies, in Cuba, and in Brazil. African slaves became the dominant source of plantation workers, as they proved more resistant to the diseases of malaria and yellow fever (European indentured servants remained in shorter supply, susceptible to disease and overall forming a less economic investment. European diseases such as smallpox had reduced the numbers of local Native Americans). But replacement of Native

American with African slaves also occurred because of the high death rates on sugar plantations. The British West Indies imported almost 4 million slaves, but had only 400,000 Blacks left after slavery ended in the British Empire in 1838.

With the European colonization of the Americas, the Caribbean became the world's largest source of sugar. These islands could supply sugarcane using slave labour and produce sugar at prices vastly lower than those of cane sugar imported from the East. Thus the economies of entire islands such as Guadaloupe and Barbados became based on sugar production. By 1750 the French colony known as Saint-Domingue (subsequently the independent country of Haiti) became the largest sugar producer in the world. Jamaica too became a major producer in the 18th century. Sugar plantations fueled a demand for manpower; between 1701 and 1810 ships brought nearly one million slaves to work in Jamaica and in Barbados.

During the eighteenth century, sugar became enormously popular. Britain, for example, consumed five times as much sugar in 1770 as in 1710. About 1750 sugar surpassed grain as "the most valuable commodity in European trade—it made up a fifth of all European imports and in the last decades of the century four-fifths of the sugar came from the British and French colonies in the West Indies." The sugar market went through a series of booms. The heightened demand and production of sugar came about to a large extent due to a great change in the eating habits of many Europeans. For example, they began consuming jams, candy, tea, coffee, cocoa, processed foods, and other sweet victuals in much greater numbers. Reacting to this increasing craze, the islands took advantage of the situation and set about producing still more sugar. In fact, they produced up to ninety percent of the sugar that the western Europeans consumed. Some islands proved more successful than others when it came to producing the product. And in Barbados and the British Leeward Islands sugar provided 93% and 97% respectively of exports.

Planters later began developing ways to boost production even more. For example, they began using more manure when growing their crops. They also developed more advanced mills and began using better types of sugarcane. In the eighteenth century "the French colonies were the most successful, especially Saint-Domingue, where better irrigation, water-power and machinery, together with concentration on newer types of sugar, increased profits. Despite these and other improvements, the price of sugar reached soaring heights, especially during events such as the revolt against the Dutch and the Napoleonic Wars. Sugar remained in high demand, and the islands' planters knew exactly how to take advantage of the situation.

As Europeans established sugar plantations on the larger Caribbean islands, prices fell, especially in Britain. By the eighteenth century all levels of society had become common consumers of the former luxury product. At first most sugar in Britain went into tea, but later confectionery and chocolates became extremely popular. Many Britons (especially children) also ate jams Suppliers commonly sold sugar in the form of a sugar loaf and consumers required sugar nips, a pliers-like tool, to break off pieces.

Sugarcane quickly exhausts the soil in which it grows, and planters pressed larger islands with fresher soil into production in the nineteenth century as demand for sugar in Europe continued to increase: "average consumption in Britain rose from four pounds per head in 1700 to eighteen pounds in 1800, 36 pounds by 1850 and over one hundred pounds by the twentieth century. In the 19th century Cuba rose to become the richest land in the Caribbean (with sugar as its dominant crop) because it formed the only major island landmass free of mountainous terrain. Instead, nearly three-quarters of its land formed a rolling plain—ideal for planting crops. Cuba also prospered above other islands because Cubans used better methods when harvesting the sugar crops: they adopted modern milling methods such as watermills, enclosed furnaces, steam engines, and vacuum-pans. All these technologies increased productivity. Cuba also retained slavery longer than the most of the rest of the Caribbean islands.

After the Haïtian Revolution established the independent State of Haiti, sugar production in that country declined and Cuba replaced Saint-Domingue as the world's largest producer.

Long established in Brazil, sugar production spread to other parts of South America, as well as to newer European colonies in Africa and in the Pacific, where it became especially important in Fiji. Mauritius, Natal and Queensland in Australia started growing sugar. The older and newer sugar-production areas now tended to use indentured labour rather than slaves, with workers "shipped across the world ... [and] ... held in conditions of near slavery for up to ten years.. In the second half of the nineteenth century over 450,000 indentured labourers went from India to the British West Indies, others went to Natal, Mauritius and Fiji (where they became a majority of the population). In Queensland workers from the Pacific islands were moved in, on Hawaii. They came from China and Japan. The Dutch transferred large numbers of people from Java to Surinam.

In Colombia, the planting of sugar started very early on, and entrepreneurs imported many African slaves to cultivate the fields. The industrialization of the Colombian industry started in 1901 with the establishment of the first steam-powered sugar mill by Santiago Eder.

While no longer grown and processed by slaves, sugar from developing countries has an ongoing association with workers earning minimal wages and living in extreme poverty

The Rise of Beet Sugar

In 1747 the German chemist Andreas Marggraf identified sucrose in beet root. This discovery remained a mere curiosity for some time, but eventually Marggraf's student Franz Achard built a sugar beet processing factory at Cunern in Silesia (in present-day Konary in Poland), under the patronage of King Frederick William III of Prussia (reigned 1797-1840). While never profitable, this plant operated from 1801 until it suffered destruction during the Napoleonic Wars (ca 1802-1815).

Napoleon, cut off from Caribbean imports by a British blockade, and at any rate not wanting to fund British merchants, banned imports of sugar in 1813. The beet-sugar industry that emerged in consequence grew, and sugar beet provides approximately 30% of world sugar production.

In the developed countries, the sugar industry relies on machinery, with a low requirement for manpower. A large beet refinery producing around 1,500 tonnes of sugar a day needs a permanent workforce of about 150 for 24-hour production.

Mechanization

Beginning in the late 18th century, the production of sugar became increasingly mechanized. The steam engine first powered a sugar mill in Jamaica in 1768, and soon after, steam replaced direct firing as the source of process heat.

In 1813 the British chemist Edward Charles Howard invented a method of refining sugar that involved boiling the cane juice not in an open kettle, but in a closed vessel heated by steam and held under partial vacuum. At reduced pressure, water boils at a lower temperature, and this development both saved fuel and reduced the amount of sugar lost through caramelization. Further gains in fuel-efficiency came from the multiple-effect evaporator, designed by the African-American engineer Norbert Rillieux (perhaps as early as the 1820s, although the first working model dates from 1845). This system consisted of a series of vacuum pans, each held at a lower pressure than the previous one. The vapors from each pan served to heat the next, with minimal heat wasted. Modern industries use multiple-effect evaporators for evaporating water.

The process of separating sugar from molasses also received mechanical attention: David Weston first applied the centrifuge to this task in Hawaii in 1852.

2 Sucrose and Glucose

Sucrose

Sucrose (common name: Table sugar, also called saccharose) is a disaccharide of glucose and fructose, with the molecular formula $C_{12}H_{22}O_{11}$. Its systematic name is a-D-glucopyranosyl- (1?2)-ß-D-fructofuranoside (ending in "oside", because it's not a reducing sugar). It is best known for its role in human nutrition and is formed by plants but not by other organisms including animals.

Physical and Chemical Properties

Pure sucrose is most often prepared as a fine, white, odorless, crystalline powder with a pleasing, sweet taste: the common table sugar. Sucrose is generally isolated from natural sources, however its chemical synthesis was first achieved in 1953 by Raymond Lemieux.

Like other carbohydrates, sucrose has a hydrogen to oxygen ratio of 2:1. It consists of two monosaccharides, a-glucose and fructose, joined by a glycosidic bond between carbon atom 1 of the glucose unit and carbon atom 2 of the fructose unit. What is notable about sucrose is that unlike most disaccharides, the glycosidic bond is formed between the reducing ends of both glucose and fructose, and not between the reducing end of one and the nonreducing end of the other. The effect of this inhibits further bonding to other saccharide units. Since it contains no anomeric hydroxyl groups, it is classified as a nonreducing sugar. Acidic hydrolysis can be used in laboratories to achieve the hydrolysis of sucrose into glucose and fructose.

Sucrose melts and decomposes at 186 °C to form caramel, and when combusted produces carbon, carbon dioxide, and water. Water breaks down sucrose by hydrolysis, however the process is so gradual that it could sit in solution for years with negligible change. If the enzyme sucrase is added however, the reaction will proceed rapidly.

Reacting sucrose with sulfuric acid dehydrates the sucrose and forms the element carbon, as demonstrated in the following equation:

$$C_{12}H_{22}O_{11} + H_2SO_4 \text{ catalyst} \rightarrow 12\,C + 11\,H_2O \qquad (2.1)$$

Commercial Production and Use

Sucrose is the most common food sweetener, although it has been replaced in American industrial food production by other sweeteners such as fructose syrups or combinations of functional ingredients and high intensity sweeteners. This is due to the subsidization of domestic sugar by the US government and an import tariff on foreign sugar, raising the price of sucrose to levels above those of the rest of the world. This makes HFCS more cost efficient for many sweetener applications.

Sugar is also used in the manufacturing of an amateur rocket motor propellant called rocket candy. In that propellant it is the fuel with potassium nitrate as the oxidizer.

Sucrose is the most important sugar in plants, and can be found in the phloem sap. It is generally extracted from sugar cane or sugar beet and then purified and crystallized. Other (minor) commercial sources are sweet sorghum and sugar maples.

Sucrose is ubiquitous in food preparations due to both its sweetness and its functional properties; it is important to the structure of many foods including biscuits and cookies, cakes and pies, candy canes, ice cream and sorbets, and also assists in the preservation of foods. As such it is common in many processed and so-called "junk foods".

Sugar as a Macronutrient

In mammals, sucrose is very readily digested in the stomach into its component sugars, by acidic hydrolysis. This step is performed by a glycoside hydrolase, which catalyzes the hydrolysis of sucrose to the monosaccharides glucose and fructose. Glucose and fructose are rapidly absorbed into the bloodstream in the small intestine. Undigested sucrose passing into the intestine is also broken down by sucrase or isomaltase glycoside hydrolases, which are located in the membrane of the microvilli lining the duodenum. These products are also transferred rapidly into the bloodstream.

Sucrose is digested by the enzyme invertase in bacteria and some animals.

In Human Nutrition

Sucrose is an easily assimilated macronutrient that provides a quick source of energy to the body, provoking a rapid rise in blood glucose upon ingestion. However, pure sucrose is not normally part of a human diet balanced for good nutrition, although it may be included sparingly to make certain foods more palatable.

Overconsumption of sucrose has been linked with some adverse health effects. The most common is dental caries or tooth decay, in which oral bacteria convert sugars (including sucrose) from food into acids that attack tooth enamel. Sucrose, as a pure carbohydrate, has an energy content of

3.94 kilocalories per gram (or 17 kilojoules per gram). When a large amount of foods that contain a high percentage of sucrose is consumed, beneficial nutrients can be displaced from the diet, which can contribute to an increased risk for chronic disease. It has been suggested that sucrose-containing drinks may be linked to the development of obesity and insulin resistance. Although most soft drinks in the USA are now made with high fructose corn syrup, not sucrose, this makes little functional difference, since high fructose corn syrup contains fructose and glucose in a similar ratio to that produced metabolically from sucrose.

The rapidity with which sucrose raises blood glucose can cause problems for people suffering from defects in glucose metabolism, such as persons with hypoglycemia or diabetes mellitus. Sucrose can contribute to the development of metabolic syndrome In an experiment with rats that were fed a diet one-third of which was sucrose, the sucrose first elevated blood levels of triglycerides, which induced visceral fat and ultimately resulted in insulin resistance. Another study found that rats fed sucrose-rich diets developed high triglycerides, hyperglycemia, and insulin resistance.

GLUCOSE

Glucose (Glc), a monosaccharide (or simple sugar) also known as grape sugar, blood sugar, or corn sugar, is a very important carbohydrate in biology. The living cell uses it as a source of energy and metabolic intermediate. Glucose is one of the main products of photosynthesis and starts cellular respiration in both prokaryotes (bacteria and archaea) and eukaryotes (animals, plants, fungi, and protists).

The name "glucose" comes from the Greek word *glykys* meaning "sweet", and the suffix "-ose," which denotes a sugar.

Two stereoisomers of the aldohexose sugars are known as glucose, only one of which (d-glucose) is biologically active. This form (d-glucose) is often referred to as dextrose monohydrate, or, especially in the food industry, simply dextrose (from *dextrorotatory glucose* This article deals with the d-form of glucose. The mirror-image of the molecule, l-glucose, cannot be metabolized by cells in the biochemical process known as glycolysis.

Structure

Glucose ($C_6H_{12}O_6$) contains six carbon atoms, one of which is part of an aldehyde group and is therefore referred to as an aldohexose. In solution, the glucose molecule can exist in an open-chain (acyclic) form and a ring (cyclic) form (in equilibrium). The cyclic form is the result of a covalent bond between the aldehyde C atom and the C-5 hydroxyl group to form a six-membered cyclic hemiacetal. At pH 7 the cyclic form is predominant. In the solid phase, glucose assumes the cyclic form. Because the ring contains five carbon atoms and one oxygen atom (like pyran), the cyclic form of glucose is also referred to as glucopyranose. In this ring, each carbon is linked to a hydroxyl side group with the exception of the fifth atom, which links to a sixth carbon atom outside the ring, forming a CH_2OH group. Glucose is commonly available in the form of a white substance or as a solid crystal. It can also be dissolved in water as an aqueous solution.

Isomers

Aldohexose sugars have four chiral centres, giving $2^4 = 16$ stereoisomers. These are split into two groups, l and d, with eight sugars in each. Glucose is one of these sugars, and l-glucose and d-glucose are two of the stereoisomers. Only seven of these are found in living organisms, of which d-glucose (Glu), d-galactose (Gal) and d-mannose (Man) are the most important. These eight isomers (including glucose itself) are related as diastereoisomers and belong to the d series.

An additional asymmetric centre at C-1 (called *the anomeric carbon atom*) is created when glucose cyclizes and two ring structures called anomers are formed as α-glucose and ß-glucose. These anomers differ structurally by the relative positioning of the hydroxyl group linked to C-1 and the group at C-6, which is termed the reference carbon. When D-glucose is drawn as a Haworth projection or in the standard chain conformation, the designation α means that the hydroxyl group attached to C-1 is positioned trans to the $-CH_2OH$ group at C-5, while ß means that it is cis. An inaccurate but superficially attractive alternative method of distinguishing α from ß is observing whether the C-1 hydroxyl is below or above the plane of the ring; this may fail if the glucose ring is drawn upside down or in an alternative chair conformation. The α and ß forms interconvert over a timescale of hours in aqueous solution, to a final stable ratio of α : ß 36:64, in a process called *mutarotation* The ratio would be α:ß 11:89 if it were not for the influence of the anomeric effect.

Rotamers

Within the cyclic form of glucose, rotation may occur around the O_6-C_6-C_5-O_5 torsion angle, termed the ω-angle, to form three rotamer conformations as shown in the diagram below. In referring to the orientations of the ω-angle and the O_6-C_6-C_5-C_4 angle, the three stable staggered rotamer conformations are termed *gauche-gauche* (gg), *gauche-trans* (gt) and *trans-gauche* (tg). For methyl α-D-glucopyranose at equilibrium the ratio of molecules in each rotamer conformation is reported as 57 : 38 : 5 gg : gt : tg. This tendency for the ω-angle to prefer to adopt a *gauche* conformation is attributed to the gauche effect.

Properties and Energy Content

The Gibbs free energy of formation of solid glucose is -909 kJ/mol, and the enthalpy of formation is -1271.1 kJ/mol. The heat of combustion (with liquid water in the product) is about 2803 kJ/mol, or 3.72 kcal per gram. The ΔG (change of Gibbs free energy) for this combustion is about -2880 kJ/mol.

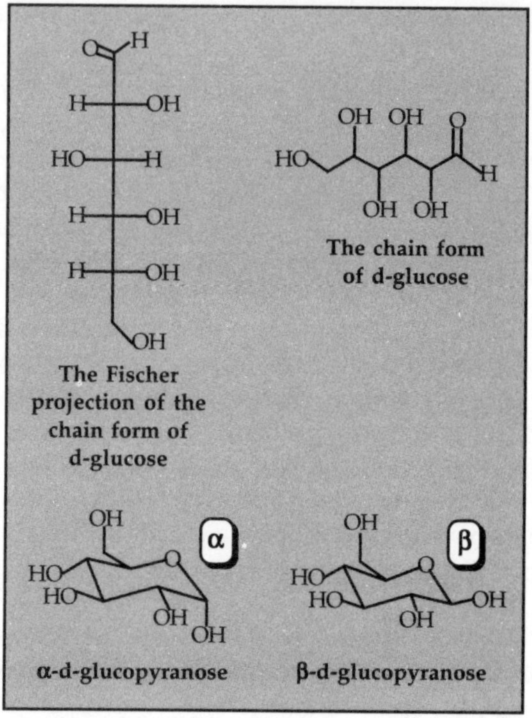

The Fischer projection of the chain form of d-glucose

The chain form of d-glucose

α-d-glucopyranose

β-d-glucopyranose

Fig. 2.1

Upon heating, glucose, like any carbohydrate, will undergo caramelization, followed by pyrolysis (carbonization) yielding steam and a char consisting mostly of carbonate. This reaction is exothermic, releasing about 0.237 kcal per gram.

Production

Natural

Glucose is one of the products of photosynthesis in plants and some prokaryotes.

In animals and fungi, glucose is the result of the breakdown of glycogen, a process known as glycogenolysis. In plants the breakdown substrate is starch.

In animals, glucose is synthesized in the liver and kidneys from non-carbohydrate intermediates, such as pyruvate and glycerol, by a process known as gluconeogenesis.

Commercial

Glucose is produced commercially via the enzymatic hydrolysis of starch. Many crops can be used as the source of starch. Maize, rice, wheat, cassava, corn husk and sago are all used in various parts of the world. In the United States, cornstarch (from maize) is used almost exclusively.

Function

Scientists can speculate on the reasons why glucose, and not another monosaccharide such as fructose (Fru), is so widely used in organisms. One reason might be that glucose has a lower tendency, as compared to other hexose sugars, to non-specifically react with the amino groups of proteins. This reaction (glycation) reduces or destroys the function of many enzymes. The low rate of glycation is due to glucose's preference for the less reactive cyclic isomer. Nevertheless, many of the long-term complications of diabetes (e.g., blindness, renal failure, and peripheral neuropathy) are probably due to the glycation of proteins or lipids. In contrast, enzyme-regulated addition of glucose to proteins by glycosylation is often essential to their function.

As an Energy Source

Glucose is a ubiquitous fuel in biology. It is used as an energy source in most organisms, from bacteria to humans. Use of glucose may be by either aerobic or anaerobic respiration (fermentation). Carbohydrates are the human body's key source of energy, through aerobic respiration, providing approximately 3.75 kilocalories (16 kilojoules) of food energy per gram. Breakdown of carbohydrates (e.g. starch) yields mono- and disaccharides, most of which is glucose. Through glycolysis and later in the reactions of the citric acid cycle (TCAC), glucose is oxidized to eventually form CO_2 and water, yielding energy sources, mostly in the form of ATP. The insulin reaction, and other mechanisms, regulate the concentration of glucose in the blood. A high fasting blood sugar level is an indication of prediabetic and diabetic conditions.

Glucose is a primary source of energy for the brain, and hence its availability influences psychological processes. When glucose is low, psychological processes requiring mental effort (e.g., self-control, effortful decision-making) are impaired

Glucose in Glycolysis

Use of glucose as an energy source in cells is via aerobic or anaerobic respiration. Both of these start with the early steps of the glycolysis metabolic pathway. The first step of this is the phosphorylation of glucose by hexokinase to prepare it for later breakdown to provide energy.

The major reason for the immediate phosphorylation of glucose by a hexokinase is to prevent diffusion out of the cell. The phosphorylation adds a charged phosphate group so the glucose 6-phosphate cannot easily cross the cell membrane. Irreversible first steps of a metabolic pathway are common for regulatory purposes.

As a Precursor

Glucose is critical in the production of proteins and in lipid metabolism. In plants and most animals, it is also a precursor for vitamin C (ascorbic acid) production. It is modified for use in these processes by the glycolysis pathway.

Glucose is used as a precursor for the synthesis of several important substances. Starch, cellulose, and glycogen ("animal starch") are common glucose polymers (polysaccharides). Lactose, the predominant sugar in milk, is a glucose-galactose disaccharide. In sucrose, another important disaccharide, glucose is joined to fructose. These synthesis processes also rely on the phosphorylation of glucose through the first step of glycolysis.

Industrial Use

In the industry glucose is used as a precursor to make vitamin C in the Reichstein process, to make citric acid, gluconic acid, bio-ethanol, polylactic acid, sorbitol.

Sources and Absorption

Most dietary carbohydrates contain glucose, either as their only building block, as in starch and glycogen, or together with another monosaccharide, as in sucrose and lactose. Crystalline fructose, for example, does not contain glucose and is about ninety-eight percent fructose. In the lumen of the duodenum and small intestine, the glucose oligo- and polysaccharides are broken down to monosaccharides by the pancreatic and intestinal glycosidases. Other polysaccarhides cannot be processed by the human intestine and require assistance by intestinal flora if they are to be broken down; the most notable exceptions are sucrose (fructose-glucose) and lactose (galactose-glucose). Glucose is then transported across the apical membrane of the enterocytes by SLC_5A_1, and later across their basal membrane by SLC_2A_2 Some of the glucose is directly utilized as an energy source by brain cells, intestinal cells and red blood cells, while the rest reaches the liver, adipose tissue and muscle cells, where it is absorbed and stored as glycogen (under the influence of insulin). Liver cell glycogen can be converted to glucose and returned to the blood when insulin is low or absent; muscle cell glycogen is not returned to the blood because of a lack of enzymes. In fat cells, glucose is used to power reactions that synthesize some fat types and have other purposes. Glycogen is the body's 'glucose energy' storage mechanism because it is much more 'space efficient' and less reactive than glucose itself.

History

Because glucose is a basic necessity of many organisms, a correct understanding of its chemical makeup and structure contributed greatly to a general advancement in organic chemistry. This understanding occurred largely as a result of the investigations of Emil Fischer, a German chemist who received the 1902 Nobel Prize in Chemistry as a result of his findings The synthesis of glucose established the structure of organic material and consequently formed the first definitive validation of Jacobus Henricus van't Hoff's theories of chemical kinetics and the arrangements of chemical bonds in carbon-bearing molecules. Between 1891 and 1894, Fischer established the stereochemical configuration of all the known sugars and correctly predicted the possible isomers, applying van't Hoff's theory of asymmetrical carbon atoms.

3 Fructose

Fructose (also levulose or laevulose) is a simple reducing sugar (monosaccharide) found in many foods and is one of the three important dietary monosaccharides along with glucose and galactose. Honey, tree fruits, berries, melons, and some root vegetables, such as beets, sweet potatoes, parsnips, and onions, contain fructose, usually in combination with glucose in the form of sucrose. Fructose is also derived from the digestion of granulated table sugar (sucrose), a disaccharide consisting of glucose and fructose, and high-fructose corn syrup (HFCS).

Crystalline fructose and high-fructose corn syrup are often mistakenly confused as the same product. The former is produced from a fructose-enriched corn syrup which results in a finished product of at least 98% fructose. The latter is usually supplied as a mixture of nearly equal amounts of fructose and glucose.

CHEMICAL PROPERTIES

Classification and Structure

Fructose, also referred to as fruit sugar is a simple monosaccharide with a ketone functional group. Fructose is an isomer of glucose with the same molecular formula ($C_6H_{12}O_6$) but with a different structure. Fructose is a 6-carbon polyhydroxyketone. When dissolved in solution, it forms ring structures similar to glucose, which are classified as cyclic hemiketals as opposed to the cyclic hemiacetals formed by aldoses such as glucose. When fructose forms a 5-member ring, the OH group on the fifth carbon atom attaches to the carbonyl group that is on the second carbon atom (D-Fructofuranose). Alternatively, the OH group on the sixth carbon may attach to the carbonyl carbon to form a 6-member ring (D-Fructopyranose). Fructose may be found at equilibrium containing a mixture of 70% fructopyranose and 30% fructofuranose.

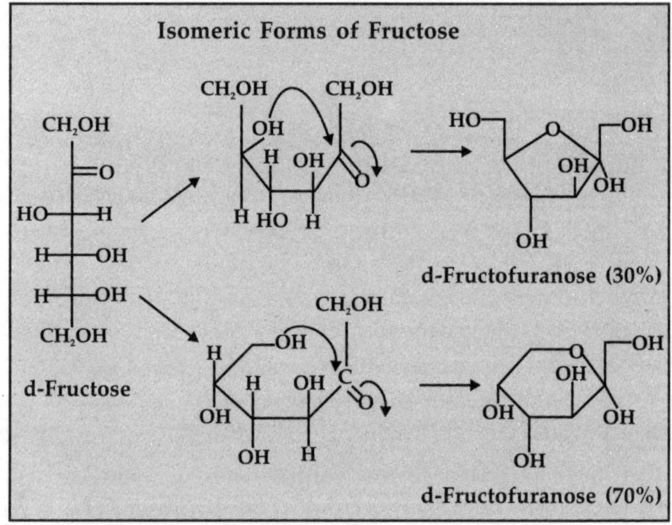

Fig. 3.1: **The cyclic hemiketal isomers of fructose**

CHEMICAL REACTIONS

Fructose and Fermentation

Fructose may be anaerobically fermented by yeast or bacteria. Yeast enzymes convert sugar (glucose, or fructose) to ethanol and carbon dioxide. The carbon dioxide released during fermentation will remain dissolved in water where it will reach equilibrium with carbonic acid unless the fermentation chamber is left open to the air. The dissolved carbon dioxide and carbonic acid produce the carbonation in bottle fermented beverages.

Fructose and Maillard Reaction

Fructose undergoes the Maillard reaction, non-enzymatic browning, with amino acids. Because fructose exists to a greater extent in the open-chain form than does glucose, the initial stages of the Maillard reaction occurs more rapidly than with glucose. Therefore, fructose potentially may contribute to changes in food palatability, as well as other nutritional effects, such as excessive browning, volume and tenderness reduction during cake preparation, and formation of mutagenic compounds.

PHYSICAL AND FUNCTIONAL PROPERTIES

Relative Sweetness

The primary reason that fructose is used commercially in foods and beverages, besides that it is inexpensive compared to sucrose, is because of its relative sweetness. It is the sweetest of all naturally occurring carbohydrates. Fructose is generally regarded as being 1.73 times sweeter than sucrose . However, it is the 5-ring form of fructose that is sweeter; the 6-ring form tastes about the same as usual table sugar. Unfortunately, warming fructose leads to formation of the 6-ring form.

The Sweetness Intensity Profile of Fructose

The sweetness of fructose is perceived earlier than that of sucrose or dextrose, and the taste sensation reaches a peak (higher than sucrose) and diminishes more quickly than sucrose. Fructose can also enhance other flavors in the system.

Sweetness Synergy

Fructose exhibits a sweetness synergy effect when used in combination with other sweeteners. The relative sweetness of fructose blended with sucrose, aspartame, or saccharin is perceived to be greater than the sweetness calculated from individual components.

Fructose Solubility and Crystallization

Fructose has the higher solubility than other sugars and sugar alcohols do. Fructose is therefore difficult to crystallize from an aqueous solution Sugar mixes containing fructose, such as candies, are softer than those containing other sugars because of the greater solubility of fructose.

Fructose Hygroscopicity and Humectancy

Fructose is quicker to absorb moisture and slower to release it to the environment than sucrose, dextrose, or other nutritive sweeteners Fructose is an excellent humectant and retains moisture for a long period of time even at low relative humidity (RH). Therefore, fructose can contribute to improved quality, better texture, and longer shelf life to the food products in which it is used.

Freezing Point

Fructose has a greater effect on freezing point depression than disaccharides or oligosaccharides, which may protect the integrity of cell walls of fruit by reducing ice crystal formation. However, this characteristic may be undesirable in soft-serve or hard-frozen dairy desserts.

FRUCTOSE AND STARCH FUNCTIONALITY IN FOOD SYSTEMS

Fructose increases starch viscosity more rapidly and achieves a higher final viscosity than sucrose because fructose lowers the temperature required during gelatinizing of starch, causing a greater final viscosity.

Food Sources

The primary food sources of fructose are fruits, vegetables, and honey Fructose exists in foods either as a free monosaccharide or bound to glucose as the disaccharide, sucrose. Fructose, glucose, and sucrose can all be present in a food; however, different foods will have varying levels of each of these three sugars.

The sugar content of common fruits and vegetables are presented in Table 3.1. In general, foods that contain free fructose have equal amount of free glucose. In other words, the ratio of fructose to glucose roughly equals 1:1. A value that is above 1 indicates higher proportion of fructose to glucose and *vice versa*. Some of the fruits have larger proportions of fructose to glucose compared to others. For example, apples and pears contain more than twice as much free fructose as glucose, while apricots contain less than a half of fructose than glucose.

Apple and pear juices are of particular interest to pediatricians due to the juices' high concentration of free fructose relative to glucose, which can cause diarrhea in children. The cells of the small intestine, enterocytes, have lower affinity for fructose absorption compared with that for glucose and sucrose. Unabsorbed fructose creates higher osmolarity in the small intestine, which draws water into the gastrointestinal tract, resulting in osmotic diarrhea. This phenomenon is discussed in greater details in Health Effects section.

Table 3.1 also shows the amount of sucrose found in common fruits and vegetables. Sugar cane and sugar beet have a high concentration of sucrose, and are used for commercial preparation of pure sucrose. Extracted cane or beet juices are clarified from the impurities and concentrated by removing excess of water. The end product is 99.9% pure sucrose. Sucrose containing sugars include common white granulated sugar, powdered sugar, as well as brown sugar.

Table 3.1: Sugar content of selected common plant foods (g/100g)

Food Item	Total Carbohydrate	Total Sugars	Free Fructose	Free Glucose	Sucrose	Fructose/ Glucose Ratio	Sucrose as a % of Total Sugars
Fruit							
Apple	13.8	10.4	5.9	2.4	2.1	2.0	19.9
Apricot	11.1	9.2	0.9	2.4	5.9	0.7	63.5
Banana	22.8	12.8	4.9	5.0	2.4	1.0	20.0
Grapes	18.1	15.5	8.1	7.2	0.2	1.1	1.0
Peach	9.5	8.4	1.5	2.0	4.8	0.9	56.7
Pear	15.5	9.8	6.2	2.8	0.8	2.1	8.0
Vegetables							
Beet, Red	9.6	6.8	0.1	0.1	6.5	1.0	96.2
Carrot	9.6	4.7	0.6	0.6	3.6	1.0	70.0
Corn, Sweet	19.0	3.2	0.5	0.5	2.1	1.0	64.0
Red Pepper, Sweet	6.0	4.2	2.3	1.9	0.0	1.2	0.0
Onion, Sweet	7.6	5.0	2.0	2.3	0.7	0.9	14.3
Sweet Potato	20.1	4.2	0.7	1.0	2.5	0.9	60.3
Yam	27.9	0.5	tr	tr	tr	na	tr
Sugar Cane		13-18	0.2-1.0	0.2-1.0	11-16	1.0	100
Sugar Beet		17-18	0.1-0.5	0.1-0.5	16-17	1.0	100

All data with a unit of g (gram) are based on 100 g of a food item. The fructose/glucose ratio is calculated by dividing the sum of free fructose plus half sucrose by the sum of free glucose plus half sucrose.

Fructose is also found in the synthetically manufactured sweetener, high-fructose corn syrup (HFCS). Hydrolyzed corn starch is used as the raw material for production of HFCS. Through the enzymatic treatment, glucose molecules are converted into fructose . There are three types of HFCS, each with a different proportion of fructose: HFCS-42, HFCS-55, and HFCS-90 (Table 3.2). The number for each HFCS corresponds to the percentage of synthesized fructose present in the syrup. HFCS-90 has the highest concentration of fructose, and is typically used to manufacture HFCS-55; HFCS 55 is used as sweetener in soft drinks, while HFCS-42 is used in many processed foods and baked goods.

Table 3.2: Commercial Sweeteners (Carbohydrate Content)

Sugar	Fructose	Glucose	Sucrose	Other Sugars
Granulated Sugar	(50)	(50)	100	0
Brown Sugar	1	1	97	1
HFCS-42	42	53	0	5
HFCS-55	55	41	0	4
HFCS-90	90	5	0	5
Honey	50	44	1	5
Maple Syrup	1	4	95	0
Molasses	23	21	53	3
Corn Syrup	0	35	0	0

However, with the development of HFCS, a significant shift occurred in the type of sweetener consumption. Contrary to the popular belief, however, with the increase of HFCS consumption, the total fructose intake has not dramatically changed. Granulated sugar is 99.9% pure sucrose, which means that it has equal ratio of fructose to glucose. The most commonly used HFCS, 42 and 55, have about equal ratio of fructose to glucose, with minor differences. HFCS has simply replaced sucrose as a sweetener. Therefore, despite the changes in the sweetener consumption, the ratio of glucose to fructose intake has remained relatively constant.

Fructose Digestion and Absorption in Humans

Fructose exists in foods as either a monosaccharide (free fructose) or as a disaccharide (sucrose). Free fructose does not undergo digestion; however when fructose is consumed in the form of sucrose, digestion occurs entirely in the upper small intestine. As sucrose comes into contact with the membrane of the small intestine, the enzyme sucrase catalyzes the cleavage of sucrose to yield one glucose and fructose unit. Fructose, passes through the small intestine, virtually unchanged, then enters the portal vein and is directed toward the liver.

The mechanism of fructose absorption in the small intestine is not completely understood. Some evidence suggests active transport, because fructose uptake has been shown to occur against a concentration gradient. However, the majority of research supports the claim that fructose absorption occurs on the mucosal membrane via facilitated transport involving GLUT5 transport proteins. Since the concentration of fructose is higher in the lumen, fructose is able to flow down a concentration gradient into the enterocytes, assisted by transport proteins. Fructose may be transported out of the enterocyte across the basolateral membrane by either GLUT2 or GLUT5, although the GLUT2 transporter has a greater capacity for transporting fructose and therefore the majority of fructose is transported out of the enterocyte through GLUT2.

Capacity and Rate of Absorption

The absorption capacity for fructose in monosaccharide form ranges from less than 5g to 50g and adapts with changes in dietary fructose intake. Studies show the greatest absorption rate occurs when glucose and fructose are administered in equal quantities When fructose is ingested as part of the disaccharide sucrose, absorption capacity is much higher because fructose exists in a 1:1 ratio with glucose. It appears that the GLUT5 transfer rate may be saturated at low levels and absorption is increased through joint absorption with glucose One proposed mechanism for this phenomenon is a glucose dependent cotransport of fructose. In addition, fructose transfer activity increases with dietary fructose intake. The presence of fructose in the lumen causes increased mRNA transcription of GLUT5, leading to increased transport proteins. High fructose diets have been shown to increase abundance of transport proteins within 3 days of intake.

Malabsorption

Several studies have measured the intestinal absorption of fructose using hydrogen breath test. These studies indicate that fructose is not completely absorbed in the small intestine. When fructose is not absorbed in the small intestine, it is transported into the large intestine, where it is fermented by the colonic flora. Hydrogen is produced during the fermentation process and dissolves into the blood of the portal vein. This hydrogen is transported to the lungs, where it is exchanged across the lungs and is measurable by the hydrogen breath test. The colonic flora also produces carbon dioxide, short chain fatty acids, organic acids, and trace gases in the presence of unabsorbed fructose The presence of gases and organic acids in the large intestine causes gastrointestinal symptoms such as bloating, diarrhea, flatulence, and gastrointestial pain Exercise can exacerbate these symptoms by decreasing transit time in the small intestine, resulting in a greater amount of fructose being emptied into the large intestine.

Fructose Metabolism

All three dietary monosaccharides are transported into the liver by the GLUT 2 transporter Fructose and galactose are phosphorylated in the liver by fructokinase (km = 0.5 mM) and galactokinase (km = 0.8 mM). By contrast, glucose tends to pass through the liver (km of hepatic glucokinase = 10 mM) and can be metabolised anywhere in the body. Uptake of fructose by the liver is not regulated by insulin.

Fructolysis

Fructolysis occurs in two steps. First, trioses, dihydroxyacetone (DHAP) and glyceraldehyde are synthesized. Second, trioses are metabolized either in the gluconeogenic pathway for glycogen replenishment and/or complete metabolism in the fructolytic pathway to pyruvate, which after conversion to acetyl-CoA enters the Krebs cycle, and is converted to citrate and subsequently directed toward "de novo" synthesis of the free fatty acid palmitate.

Metabolism of Fructose to DHAP and Glyceraldehyde

The first step in the metabolism of fructose is the phosphorylation of fructose to fructose 1-phosphate by fructokinase, thus trapping fructose for metabolism in the liver. Fructose 1-phosphate then undergoes hydrolysis by aldolase B to form DHAP and glyceraldehydes; DHAP can either be isomerized to glyceraldehyde 3-phosphate by triosephosphate isomerase or undergo reduction to glycerol 3-phosphate by glycerol 3-phosphate dehydrogenase. The glyceraldehyde produced may also be converted to glyceraldehyde 3-phosphate by glyceraldehyde kinase or converted to glycerol 3-phosphate by glyceraldehyde 3-phosphate dehydrogenase. The metabolism of fructose at this point yields intermediates in the gluconeogenic and fructolytic pathways leading to glycogen synthesis as well as fatty acid and triglyceride synthesis.

Synthesis of Glycogen from DHAP and Glyceraldehyde 3 Phosphate

The resultant glyceraldehyde formed by aldolase B then undergoes phosphorylation to glyceraldehyde 3-phosphate. Increased concentrations of DHAP and glyceraldehyde 3-phosphate in the liver drive the gluconeogenic pathway toward glucose and subsequent glycogen synthesis. It appears that fructose is a better substrate for glycogen synthesis than glucose and that glycogen replenishment takes precedence over triglyceride formation Once liver glycogen is replenished, the intermediates of fructose metabolism are primarily directed toward triglyceride synthesis.

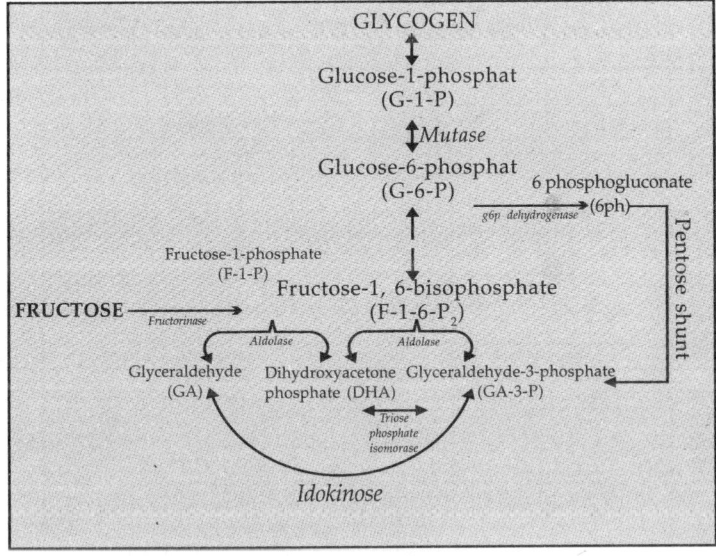

Fig. 3.2: **Metabolic conversion of fructose to glycogen in the liver**

Synthesis of Triglyceride from DHAP and Glyceraldehyde 3 Phosphate

Carbons from dietary fructose are found in both the free fatty acid and glycerol moieties of plasma triglycerides.

High fructose consumption can lead to excess pyruvate production, causing a buildup of Krebs cycle intermediates . Accumulated citrate can be transported from the mitochondria into the cytosol of hepatocytes, converted to acetyl CoA by citrate lyase and directed toward fatty acid synthesis . Additionally, DHAP can be converted to glycerol 3-phosphate as previously mentioned, providing the glycerol backbone for the triglyceride molecule Triglycerides are incorporated into very low density lipoproteins (VLDL), which are released from the liver destined toward peripheral tissues for storage in both fat and muscle cells.

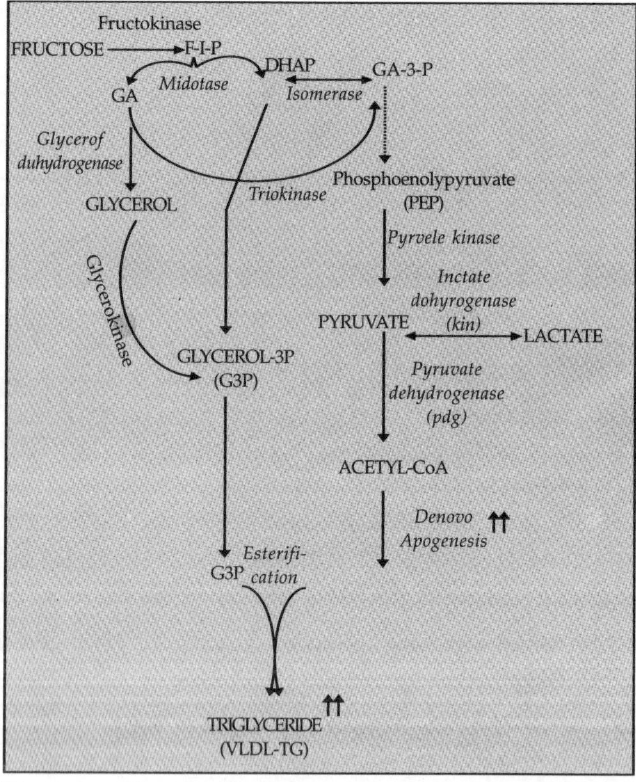

Fig. 3.3: Metabolic conversion of fructose to triglyceride in the liver

Health Effects

Fructose absorption occurs via the GLUT 5 (fructose only) transporter, and the GLUT2 transporter, for which it competes with glucose and galactose. A deficiency of GLUT 5 may result in excess fructose carried into the lower intestine There, it can provide nutrients for the existing gut flora, which produce gas. It may also cause water retention in the intestine. These effects may lead to bloating, excessive flatulence, loose stools, and even diarrhea depending on the amounts eaten and other factors.

Excess fructose consumption has been hypothesized to be a contributing cause of insulin resistance, obesity, elevated LDL cholesterol and triglycerides, leading to metabolic syndrome Short-term tests, lack of dietary control, and lack of a non-fructose consuming control group are all confounding factors in human experiments. However, there are now a number of reports showing correlation of fructose consumption to obesity, especially central obesity which is thought to be the most dangerous kind of obesity.

There is a concern with Type 1 diabetes patients and the apparent low GI (glycemic index) of fructose. Fructose gives as high a blood sugar spike as that obtained with glucose. In fact, the GI measurement applies only to glucose containing foods (e.g., those with high-starch content). The basic GI measurement technique is somewhat confusing. This is because the body's response to glucose is "standardized" with 50g of ingested glucose, while the GI researchers use 50g of digestible carbohydrate (not necessarily glucose) as its reference standard. Although all simple sugars have nearly identical chemical formulae, each has distinct chemical properties. This can be illustrated with pure fructose. A journal article reports that, ". . .fructose given alone increased the blood glucose almost as much as a similar amount of glucose (78% of the glucose-alone area)". A study in mice suggests that fructose increases the risk of obesity.

One study concluded that fructose "produced significantly higher fasting plasma triacylglycerol values than did the glucose diet in men" and ". . .if plasma triacylglycerols are a risk factor for cardiovascular disease, then diets high in fructose may be undesirable" Bantle et al. "noted the same effects in a study of 14 healthy volunteers who sequentially ate a high-fructose diet and one almost devoid of the sugar."

Studies that have compared high fructose corn syrup (an ingredient in nearly all soft drinks sold in the US) to sucrose (common table sugar) find that most measured physiological effects are equivalent. For instance the effects of HFCS and sucrose sweetened drinks on blood glucose, insulin, leptin, and ghrelin levels. It is found no significant differences in any of these parameters This is not surprising since sucrose is a disaccharide which digests to 50% glucose and 50% fructose; while the high fructose corn syrup most commonly used on soft drinks is 55% fructose. The difference between the two lies in the fact that HFCS contains little sucrose, the fructose and glucose being independent moities.

Fructose is often recommended for diabetics because it does not trigger the production of insulin by pancreatic ß cells, probably because ß cells have low levels of GLUT5 . Fructose has a very low glycemic index of 19 ± 2, compared with 100 for glucose and 68 ± 5 for sucrose. Fructose is also seventy-three percent sweeter than sucrose at room temperature, so diabetics can use less of it. Studies show that fructose consumed before a meal may even lessen the glycemic response of the meal Its sweetness changes at higher temperatures, so its effects in recipes are not equivalent to sucrose (i.e., table sugar).

Every cell in the body can metabolize glucose. However, all fructose must be metabolized in the liver. The livers of the rats on the high fructose diet looked like the livers of alcoholics, plugged with fat and cirrhotic. This is not entirely true as a few other tissues (eg, sperm cells and some intestinal cells) do use fructose directly, though in less metabolically significant amounts.

Fructose is a reducing sugar, as are all monosaccharides. The spontaneous chemical reaction of simple sugar molecules to proteins, known as glycation, is thought to be a significant cause of damage in diabetics. Fructose appears to be equivalent to glucose in this regard and so does not seem to be a better answer for diabetes for this reason alone, save for the smaller quantities required to achieve equivalent sweetness in some foods. This may be an important contribution to senescence and many age-related chronic diseases.

Fructose is used as a substitute for sucrose (composed of one unit each of fructose and glucose linked together with a relatively weak glycosidic bond) because it is less expensive for a given degree of sweetness and has little effect on measured blood glucose levels. Often, fructose is consumed as high fructose corn syrup, which is corn syrup (glucose) that has been enzymatically treated by the enzyme glucose isomerase to increase the concentration of fructose. This enzyme converts a portion of the glucose into fructose thus making it taste sweeter. This is done to such a degree as to yield corn syrup with an equivalent sweetness to sucrose by weight (the chief sugar in corn syrup is the significantly less sweet glucose). While most carbohydrates have around the same amount of calories, fructose is sweeter than others and manufacturers can use less of it to get the same result. The free fructose present in fruits, their juices, and honey is responsible for the sometimes intense sweetness of these natural sugar sources.

Unlike glucose, fructose is almost entirely metabolized in the liver. "When fructose reaches the liver," says Dr. William J. Whelan, a biochemist at the University of Miami School of Medicine, "the liver goes bananas and stops everything else to metabolize the fructose." Eating fructose as compared to glucose results in lower circulating insulin (pancreatic beta cell insulin release is controlled only by blood glucose levels) and leptin levels, and attenuation in the suppression of ghrelin postprandially These hormones are implicated in the control of appetite and satiety, and it is suspected that eating large amounts of fructose increases the likelihood of weight gain. elieved to contribute to the development of non-alcoholic fatty liver disease

It has been suggested in a recent *British Medical Journal* study that high consumption of fructose is even linked to gout. Cases of gout have risen in recent years, despite commonly being thought of as a Victorian disease, and it is suspected that the fructose found in soft drinks (e.g, carbonated beverages) and other sweetened drinks is the reason for this.

4 Monosaccharide

Monosaccharides (from Greek *monos*: single, *sacchar*: sugar) are the most basic unit of carbohydrates. They are the simplest form of sugar and are usually colorless, water-soluble, crystalline solids. Some monosaccharides have a sweet taste. Examples of monosaccharides include glucose (dextrose), fructose (levulose), galactose, xylose and ribose. Monosaccharides are the building blocks of disaccharides such as sucrose and polysaccharides (such as cellulose and starch). Further, each carbon atom that supports a hydroxyl group (except for the first and last) is chiral, giving rise to a number of isomeric forms all with the same chemical formula. For instance, galactose and glucose are both aldohexoses, but have different chemical and physical properties.

Structure

With few exceptions (e.g., deoxyribose), monosaccharides have the chemical formula $C_x(H_2O)_y$ with the chemical structure $H(CHOH)_nC{=}O(CHOH)_mH$. If n or m is zero, it is an aldehyde and is termed an aldose, otherwise it is a ketone and is termed a ketose. Monosaccharides contain either a ketone or aldehyde functional group, and hydroxyl groups on most or all of the non-carbonyl carbon atoms.

Cyclic Structure

Most monosaccharides will cyclize in aqueous solution, forming hemiacetals or hemiketals (depending on whether they are aldoses or ketoses) between an alcohol and the carbonyl group of the same sugar. Glucose, for example, readily forms a hemiacetal linkage between its carbon[1] and oxygen[5] to form a 6-membered ring called a pyranoside. The same reaction can take place between carbon[1] and oxygen[4] to form a 5-membered furanoside. In general, pyranosides are more stable and are the major form of the monosaccharide observed in solution. Since cyclization forms a new stereogenic center at carbon1, two anomers can be formed (α-isomer and ß-isomer) from each distinct straight-chain monosaccharide. The interconversion between these two forms is called mutarotation.

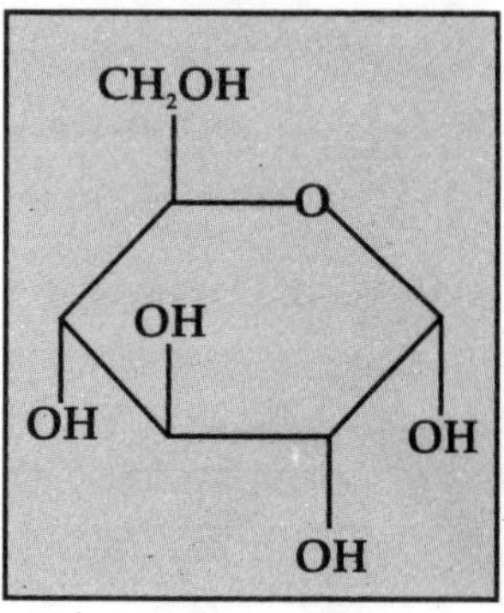

Fig. 4.1: α-d-Glucopyranose (Haworth projection)

A common way of representing the structure of monosaccharides is the Haworth projection. In a Haworth projection, the α-isomer has the OH- of the anomeric carbon below the plane of the carbon atoms, and the ß-isomer, has the OH- of the anomeric carbon above the plane. Monosaccharides typically adopt a chair conformation, similar to cyclohexane. In this conformation the α-isomer has

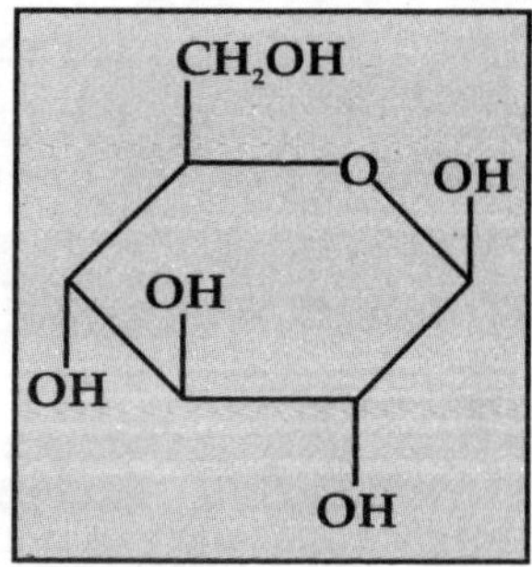

Fig. 4.2: ß-d-Glucopyranose (Haworth projection)

the OH- of the anomeric carbon in an axial position, whereas the ß-isomer has the OH- of the anomeric carbon in equatorial position.

Monosaccharides are the basic unit of carbohydrates, which cannot be further hydrolysed in to simpler units. Depending on the number of carbon atom they are further classified in to trioses, tetroses, pentoses, hexoses etc, which is further classified in to aldoses and ketoses depending on the type of functional group present in them.

Monosaccharides are classified the type of carbonyl group they contain:

- Aldose, -CHO (aldehyde) and;
- Ketose, C=O (ketone)

Isomerism

The total number of possible stereoisomers of one compound (n) is dependent on the number of stereogenic centers (c) in the molecule. The upper limit for the number of possible stereoisomers is $n = 2^c$. The only carbohydrate without an isomer is dihydroxyacetone or DHA.

Monosaccharides are classified according to their molecular configuration at the chiral carbon furthest removed from the aldehyde or ketone group. The chirality at this carbon is compared to the chirality of carbon 2 on glyceraldehyde. If it is equivalent to d-glyceraldehyde's C2, the sugar is d; if it is equivalent to L-glyceraldehyde's C2, the sugar is l. Due to the chirality of the sugar molecules, an aqueous solution of a d or l saccharides will rotate light. d-glyceraldehyde causes polarized light to rotate clockwise (dextrorotary); l-glyceraldehyde causes polarized light to rotate counterclockwise (levorotary). Unlike glyceraldehyde, d/l designation on more complex sugars is not associated with their direction of light rotation. Since more complex sugars contain multiple chiral carbons, the direction of light rotation cannot be predicted by the chirality of the carbon that defines d/l nomenclature.

- d, configuration as in d- glyceraldehyde
- L, configuration as in L- glyceraldehyde

All these classifications can be combined, resulting in names like d-*aldohexose* or *ketotriose.*

Derivatives

A large number of biologically important modified monosaccharides exist:

Amino sugars such as:

- Galactosamine
- Glucosamine
- Sialic acid
- *N*-Acetylglucosamine

Sulfosugars such as:

- Sulfoquinovose

Pyranose

It is a collective term for carbohydrates which have a chemical structure that includes a six-membered ring consisting of five carbon atoms and one oxygen atom. The name derives from its similarity to the oxygen hete o-cycle pyran.

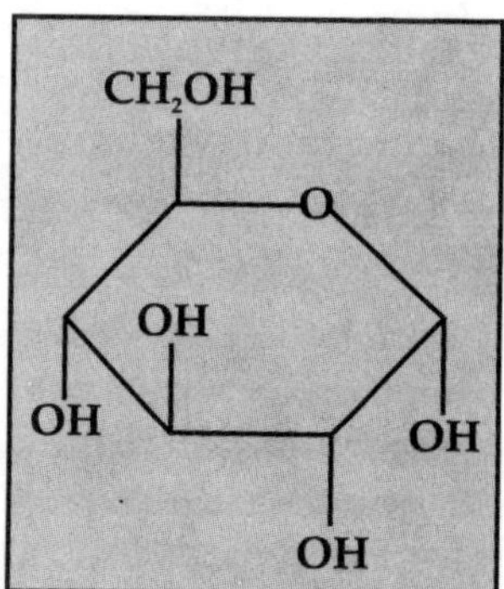

Fig. 4.3: α-*d-Glucopyranose*

Formation of Pyranose

The pyranose ring is formed by the reaction of the hydroxyl group on carbon 5 (C-5) of a sugar with the aldehyde at carbon 1. This forms an intramolecular hemiacetal. If reaction is between the C-4 hydroxyl and the aldehyde, a furanose is formed instead. The pyranose form is thermodynamically more stable than the furanose form, which can be seen by the distribution of these two cyclic forms in solution.

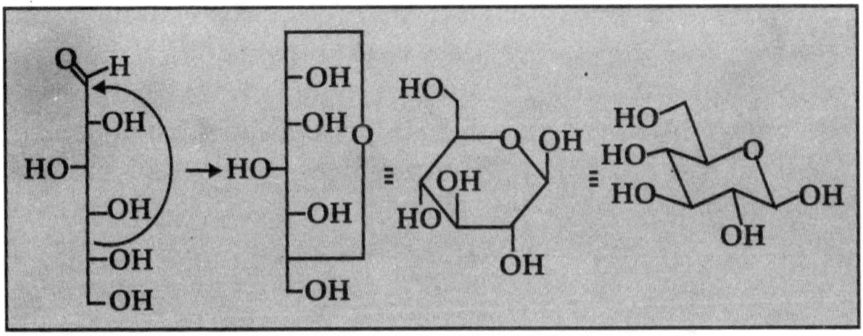

Fig. 4.4: **Formation of pyranose hemiacetal and representations of beta-D-glucopyranose**

History

Hermann Emil Fischer won the Nobel Prize in Chemistry (1902) for his work in determining the structure of the D-aldohexoses. However, the linear, free-aldehyde structures that Fischer proposed represent a very minor percentage of the forms that hexose sugars adopt in solution. It was Edmund Hirst and Clifford Purves, in the research group of Walter Haworth, who conclusively determined that the hexose sugars preferentially form a pyranose, or six-membered, ring. Haworth drew the ring as a flat hexagon with groups above and below the plane of the ring – the Haworth projection.

A further refinement to the conformation of pyranose rings came when Sponsler and Dore (1926) realized that Sachse's mathematical treatment of six-membered rings could be applied to their X-ray structure of cellulose It was determined that the pyranose ring is puckered, to allow all of the carbon atoms of the ring to have close to the ideal tetrahedral geometry.

Conformation of the Pyranose Ring

This puckering leads to a total of 38 distinct basic pyranose conformations: 2 chairs, 6 boats, 6 skew-boats, 12 half-chairs, and 12 envelopes.

These conformers can interconvert with one another; however, each form may have very different relative energy, so a significant barrier to interconversion may be present. The energy of these conformations can be calculated from quantum mechanics; an example of possible glucopyranose interconversions is given.

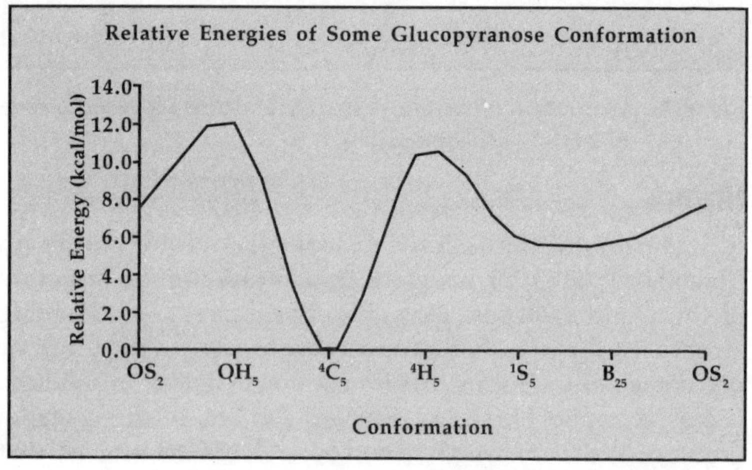

Fig. 4.5: **Relative energy of β-d-glucopyranose conformers**

The conformations of the pyranose ring are superficially similar to that of the cyclohexane ring. However, the specific nomenclature of pyranoses includes reference to the ring oxygen and the presence of hydroxyls on the ring have distinct effects on its conformational preference. There are also conformational and stereochemical effects specific to the pyranose ring.

Nomenclature of Pyranose Rings

To name conformations of pyranose, first the conformer is determined. The common conformers are similar to those found in cyclohexane, and these form the basis of the name. Common conformations are Chair (C), Boat (B), Skew (S), Half-Chair (H) or Envelope (E). The ring atoms are then numbered; the anomeric, or hemiacetal, carbon is always 1.

Oxygen atoms in the structure are generally referred to by the carbon atom they are attached to in the acyclic form, and designated O. Then:

- Position the ring so that, if looking at the top face, the atoms are numbered clockwise. 4 (or 5, in the case of an envelope) atoms will be in a plane.
- Atoms above the plane are written before the conformer label, as a superscript.
- Atoms below the plane are written following the conformer label, as a subscript.

NMR Spectroscopy of Pyranose Rings

As shown by the relative structure energies in the diagram above, the chair structures are the most stable carbohydrate form. This relatively defined and stable conformation means that the hydrogen atoms of the pyranose ring are held at relatively constant angles to one another. Carbohydrate NMR takes advantage of these dihedral angles to determine the configuration of each of the hydroxyl groups around the ring.

Monosaccharide Nomenclature

Monosaccharides are classified by the number of carbon atoms they contain:

- Triose, 3 carbon atoms
- Tetrose, 4 carbon atoms
- Pentose, 5 carbon atoms
- Hexose, 6 carbon atoms
- Heptose, 7 carbon atoms.

General Formula of Carbohydrates

Carbohydrates have the general formula $C_n(H_2O)_n$ with one degree of unsaturation, where n is the number of carbon atoms present in the structure.

Existence in Solution

In solution carbohydrates exist as an equilibrium mixture between acyclic and cyclic (pyranose and furanose) forms.

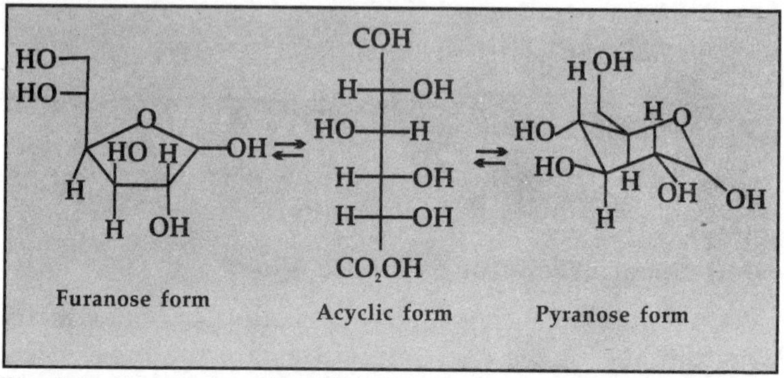

Furanose form   Acyclic form   Pyranose form

Fig. 4.6: **Interconversion between the pyranose, acyclic, and furanose forms**

Chair Conformation of Pentoses and Hexoses

Structure of d-pentoses

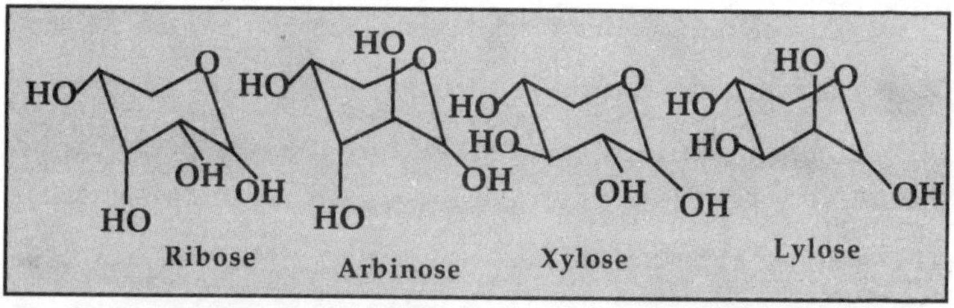

Ribose   Arbinose   Xylose   Lylose

Fig. 4.7: **Pyranose forms of some pentose sugars**

δ and L Configuration

δ and l configurations are assigned to monosaccharides depending on spatial configuration of hydroxyl group present on the stereogenic centre furthest from the carbonyl group. If –OH group is present on the right hand side in Fischer projection, configuration is assigned as D and if –OH group is present on the left hand side then configuration is assigned as L.

Structure of δ-hexoxes

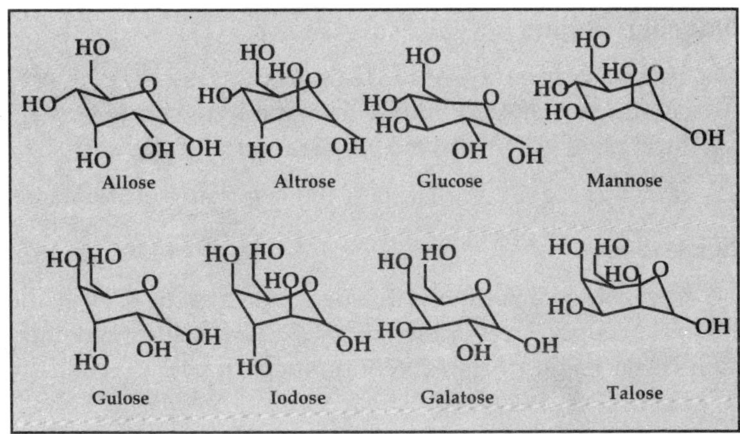

Fig. 4.8: **Pyranose forms of some hexose sugars**

Acyclic Sugars

(a) Chains are numbered in such a way that carbonyl group get the lowest number (if carbonyl group is aldehyde that type of sugars is falls under aldoses whereas if carbonyl group is ketone, then they categorized as ketoses).

(b) Rotate the molecule such that carbonyl group is as close to the top as possible.

(c) Specify the number of carbon atoms (tri, tetra, penta etc).

(d) Specify the site of oxidation (-ose, -ulose). (In ketones, if carbonyl is present at any other position other than C-2 then indicates the position of carbonyl).

(e) Specify the absolute configuration of stereogenic centre furthest from carbonyl group as δ and l.

(f) Specify the relative configurations of the other –OH groups with trivial name prefixes (gluco, manno, galacto etc).

NOMENCLATURE OF CYCLIC SUGARS

Reducing Sugars

(a) In cyclic sugars prefix designating ring size (furan, pyran, septan etc) added to name between the prefix indicating the relative configuration and the suffix.

(b) α or ß designation placed at the beginning of the name.

Glycosides

Glycosides are the cyclic sugars in which –OH at the anomeric centre is replaced with -OR. Glycosides generally have three basic units- glycone (sugar part), glycosisdic oxygen and aglycone (non-sugar group).

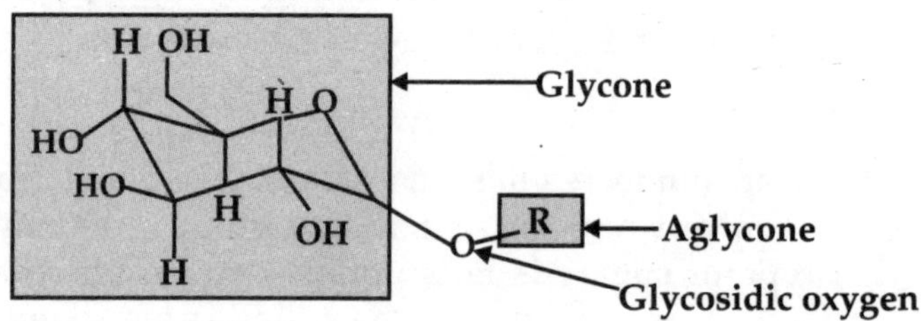

Fig. 4.9

Nomenclature of Glycosides

Glycosides are named by replacing –e ending by –ide and put the aglyconic alcohol name at front.

Modified Sugars

Modification of sugar is generally done by replacing one or more –OH group with other functional groups at all position except C-1. Since all these cases involves the removal of an –OH group, they are all deoxy sugars.

Rules for Nomenclature of Modified Sugars:

1. State the Sugar is deoxy sugar.
2. Specify the position of deoxygenation.

3. If there is a substituent other than H in the place of –OH, specify what it is.
4. Specify the relative configuration of all stereogenic centres (manno, gluco etc).
5. Specify the ring size (furanose, pyranose etc) and anomeric configuration (a or b).
6. State the chain length only in situation where –OH is replaced with H.
7. Alphabetize all the substituent groups (deoxy, -iodo, -amino etc). Di-, tri- etc prefixes do not count.

Protected Sugars

Sugars in which –OH is protected by some modification are called protected sugars.

Rules for Nomenclature for Protected Sugars

1. Specify the number of particular protecting groups (di, tri, tetra etc).
2. List groups alphabetically along with all other substituents (di, tri prefixes do not count).

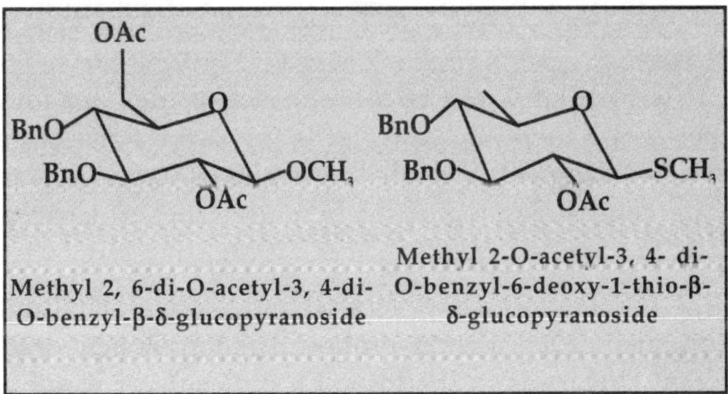

Fig. 4.10

DISACCHARIDE

A disaccharide is a sugar (a carbohydrate) composed of two monosaccharides.

'Disaccharide' is one of the four chemical groupings of carbohydrates (monosaccharide, disaccharide, oligosaccharide, and polysaccharide).

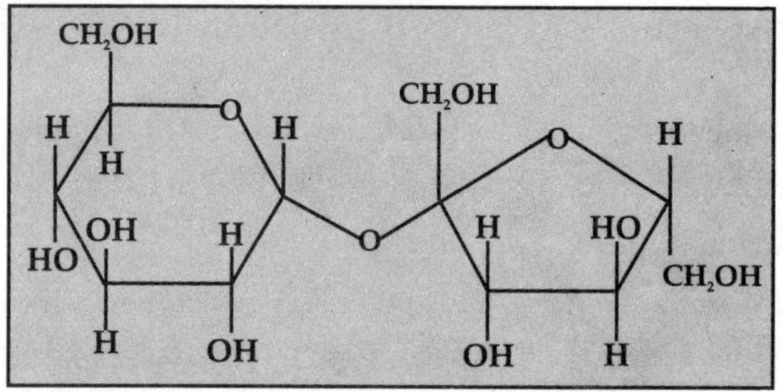

Fig. 4.11: **Sucrose, a common disaccharide**

Classification

There are two basic types of disaccharides: reducing disaccharides, in which the monosaccharide components are bonded by hydroxyl groups; and non-reducing disaccharides, in which the components bond through their anometric centers.

It is formed when two monosaccharides are joined together and a molecule of water is removed. For example; milk sugar (lactose) is made from glucose and galactose whereas cane sugar (sucrose) is made from glucose and fructose.

The two monosaccharides are bonded via a dehydration reaction (also called a condensation reaction or dehydration synthesis) that leads to the loss of a molecule of water and formation of a glycosidic bond.

Properties

The glycosidic bond can be formed between any hydroxyl group on the component monosaccharide. So, even if both component sugars are the same (e.g., glucose), different bond combinations (regiochemistry) and stereochemistry (*alpha-* or *beta-*) result in disaccharides that are diastereoisomers with different chemical and physical properties.

Depending on the monosaccharide constituents, disaccharides are sometimes crystalline, sometimes water-soluble, and sometimes sweet-tasting and sticky-feeling.

Common Disaccharides

Disaccharide	Unit 1	Unit 2	Bond
Sucrose (*table sugar, cane sugar, saccharose* or *beet sugar*)	glucose	fructose	α (1 → 2)
Lactose (*milk sugar*)	galactose	glucose	ß (1 → 4)
Maltose	glucose	glucose	α (1 → 4
Trehalose	glucose	glucose	α (1 → 1)α
Cellobiose	glucose	glucose	ß (1 → 4)

Maltose and cellobiose are hydrolysis products of the polysaccharides, starch and cellulose, respectively.

5 Oligosaccharide

An oligosaccharide is a saccharide polymer containing a small number (typically three to ten of component sugars, also known as simple sugars. The name derived from the Greek *oligos*, meaning "a few".

They are generally found either *O*- or *N*-linked to compatible amino acid side chains in proteins or to lipid moieties (see glycans).

Examples

Fructo-oligosaccharides (FOS), which are found in many vegetables, consist of short chains of fructose molecules. Inulin has a much higher degree of polymerization than FOS and is a polysaccharide. Galactooligosaccharides (GOS), which also occur naturally, consist of short chains of galactose molecules. These compounds can be only partially digested by humans.

Oligosaccharides are often found as a component of glycoproteins or glycolipids and as such are often used as chemical markers, often for cell recognition. An example is

ABO blood type specificity. A and B blood types have two different oligosaccharide glycolipids embedded in the cell membranes of the red blood cells, AB-type blood has both, while O blood type has neither.

Mannan-oligosaccharides (MOS) are widely used in animal feed to encourage gastrointestinal health and performance. They are normally obtained from the yeast cell walls of *Saccharomyces cerevisiae*. Some brand names are: CitriStim, Bio-Mos, SAF-Mannan, Y-MOS and Celmanax.

Therapeutic Effects

When oligosaccharides are consumed, the undigested portion serves as food for the intestinal microflora. Depending on the type of oligosaccharide, different bacterial groups are stimulated or suppressed.

Clinical studies have shown that administering FOS, GOS, or inulin can increase the number of these friendly bacteria in the colon while simultaneously reducing the population of harmful bacteria.

Other benefits noted with FOS, GOS, or inulin supplementation include increased production of beneficial short-chain fatty acids such as butyrate, increased absorption of calcium and magnesium, and improved elimination of toxic compounds.

Because FOS, GOS, and inulin improve colon function and may influence the bacterial composition, one might expect these compounds would help relieve the symptoms of irritable bowel syndrome. However, a double-blind trial found no clear benefit with FOS supplementation (2 grams three times daily) in patients with this condition.

Experimental studies with FOS in animals suggest a possible benefit in lowering blood sugar levels in people with diabetes and in reducing elevated blood cholesterol and triglyceride levels

In a double-blind trial of middle-aged men and women with elevated cholesterol and triglyceride levels, supplementation with inulin (10 grams per day for eight weeks) significantly reduced insulin concentrations, suggesting an improvement in blood-glucose control, and significantly lowered triglyceride levels.

In a preliminary trial, administration of FOS (8 grams per day for two weeks) significantly lowered fasting blood-sugar levels and serum total-cholesterol levels in patients with type 2 (non-insulin-dependent) diabetes.

However, in another trial, people with type 2 diabetes supplementing with FOS (15 grams per day) for 20 days found no effect on blood-glucose or lipid levels. Because of these conflicting results, more research is needed to determine the effect of FOS and inulin on diabetes and lipid levels.

Several double-blind trials have looked at the ability of FOS or inulin to lower blood cholesterol and triglyceride levels. These trials have shown that in people with elevated total cholesterol or triglyceride levels, including people with type 2 (adult onset) diabetes, FOS or inulin (in amounts ranging from 8 to 20 grams daily) produced significant reductions in triglyceride levels. However, the effect on cholesterol levels was inconsistent. In people with normal or low cholesterol or triglyceride levels, FOS or inulin produced little effect.

Sources

The FOS and inulin are found naturally in Jerusalem artichoke, burdock, chicory, leeks, onions, and asparagus. FOS products derived from chicory root contain significant quantities of inulin, a fiber widely distributed in fruits, vegetables and plants. Inulin is a significant part of the daily diet of most of the world's population. FOS can also be synthesized by enzymes of the fungus *Aspergillus niger* acting on sucrose. The GOS is naturally found in soybeans and can be synthesized from lactose (milk sugar). FOS, GOS, and inulin are available as nutritional supplements in capsules, tablets, and as a powder.

Not all natural oligosaccharides occur as components of glycoproteins or glycolipids. Some, such as the raffinose series, occur as storage or transport carbohydrates in plants. Others, such as maltodextrins or cellodextrins, result from the microbial breakdown of larger polysaccharides such as starch or cellulose.

Oligosaccharide Nomenclature

Oligosaccharides and polysaccharides are an important class of polymeric carbohydrates found in virtually all living entities. Their structural features make their nomenclature challenging and their roles in living systems make their nomenclature important.

OLIGOSACCHARIDE AND POLYSACCHARIDE NOMENCLATURE

Oligosaccharides

Oligosaccharides are carbohydrates that are composed of several monosaccharide residues joined through glycosidic linkage, which can be hydrolyzed by acid to give the constituent monosaccharide units While a strict definition of an oligosaccharide is not established, it is generally agreed that a carbohydrate consisting of two to ten monosaccharide residues with a defined structure is an oligosaccharide.

Some oligosaccharides, for example maltose, sucrose, and lactose, were trivially named before their chemical constitution was determined, and these names are still used today.

Trivial names, however, are not useful for most other oligosaccharides and, as such, systematic rules for the nomenclature of carbohydrates have been developed. To fully understand oligosaccharide and polysaccharide, one must understand how monosaccharides are named.

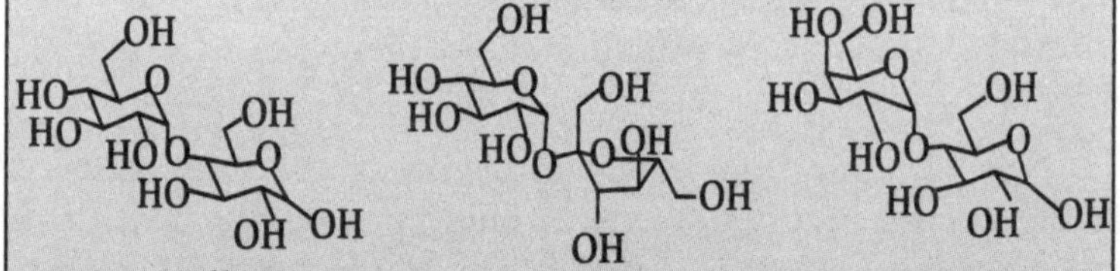

Mallose Sucrose Lactose

Fig. 5.1

An oligosaccharide contains both a reducing and non-reducing end. The reducing end of an oligosaccharide is the monosaccharide residue bearing the hemiacetal functionality, thereby capable of reducing the Tollens' reagent while the non-reducing end is the monosaccharide residue tied up as the acetal and thus incapable of reducing the Tollens' reagent The reducing and non-reducing ends of an oligosaccharide, by convention, are drawn with the monosaccharide residue furthest to the right as the reducing end and furthest to the left, the non-reducing (or terminal) end.

Naming of oligosaccharides is done from left to right as glycosyl [glycosyl]n glycoses or glycosyl [glycosyl]n glycosides, depending on whether the reducing end is a free hemiacetal group In parentheses, between the names of the monosaccharide residues, the number of the anomeric carbon atom, an arrow, and the number of the carbon atom bearing the connecting oxygen of the next monosaccharide unit are listed. Appropriate symbols are used to indicate the stereochemistry of the glycosidic bonds (α or ß), the configuration of the monosaccharide residue (δ or l), and the substitutions at oxygen atoms (O). For example, maltose and a derivative of sucrose illustrate these concepts.

In the case of branched oligosaccharides, meaning that the structure contains at least one monosaccharide residue linked to more than two other monosaccharide residues. Terms designating the branches should be listed in square brackets, with the longest linear chain, the parent chain, written without square brackets The following example will help illustrate this concept.

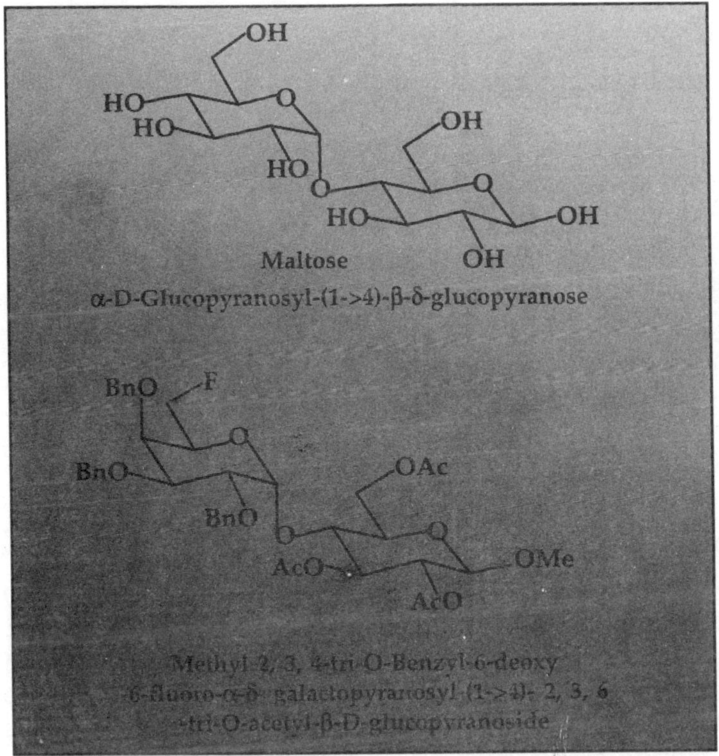

Maltose

α-D-Glucopyranosyl-(1->4)-β-δ-glucopyranose

Methyl 2, 3, 4-tri-O-Benzyl-6-deoxy 6-fluoro-α-δ-galactopyranosyl-(1->4)-2, 3, 6 tri-O-acetyl-β-D-glucopyranoside

Fig. 5.2

These systematic names are quite useful in that they provide information about the structure of the oligosaccharide. They do require a lot of space, however. As such, the abbreviated forms of the names are used when possible In these abbreviated forms, the names of the monosaccharide units are shortened to their corresponding three letter abbreviations, followed by "p" for pyranose or "f" for furanose ring structures, with the abbreviated aglyconic alcohol placed at the end of the name. Using this abbreviated system, the previous example would have the following abbreviated name.

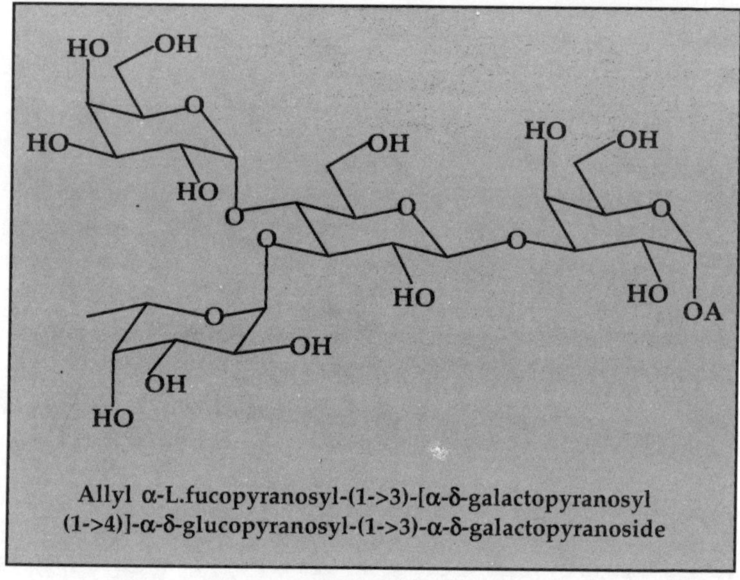

Allyl α-L.fucopyranosyl-(1->3)-[α-δ-galactopyranosyl (1->4)]-α-δ-glucopyranosyl-(1->3)-α-δ-galactopyranoside

Fig. 5.3

Polysaccharides

Polysaccharides are considered to be polymers of monosaccharides containing ten or more monosaccharide residues Polysaccharides have been given trivial names that reflect their origin. Two common examples are cellulose, a main component of the cell wall in plants, and starch, a name derived from the Anglo-Saxon stercan, meaning to stiffen.

To name a polysaccharide composed of a single type of monosaccharide, that is a homopolysaccharide, the ending "-ose" of the monosaccharide is replaced with "-an". For example, a glucose polymer is named glucan, a mannose polymer is named mannan, and a galactose polymer is named galactan. When the glycosidic linkages and configurations of the monosaccharides are known, they may be included as a prefix to the name, with the notation for glycosidic linkages preceding the symbols designating the configuration The following example will help illustrate this concept.

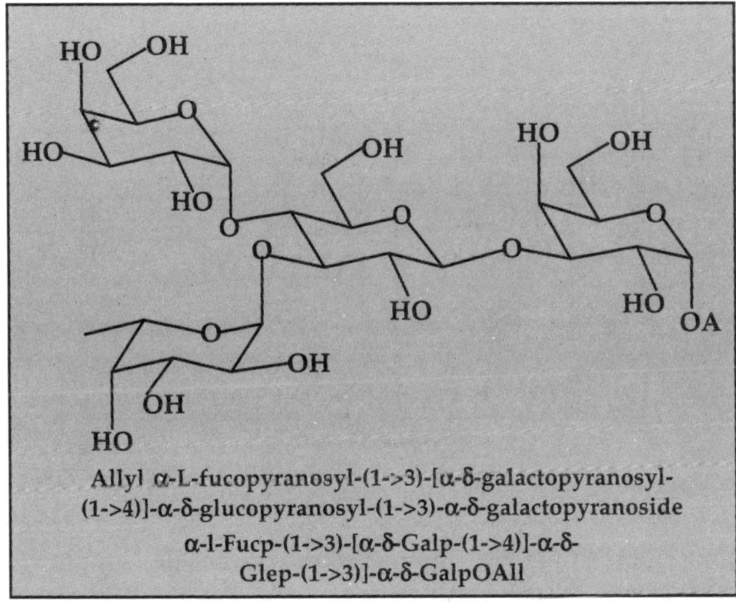

Allyl α-L-fucopyranosyl-(1->3)-[α-δ-galactopyranosyl-(1->4)]-α-δ-glucopyranosyl-(1->3)-α-δ-galactopyranoside

α-l-Fucp-(1->3)-[α-δ-Galp-(1->4)]-α-δ-Glcp-(1->3)]-α-δ-GalpOAll

Fig. 5.4

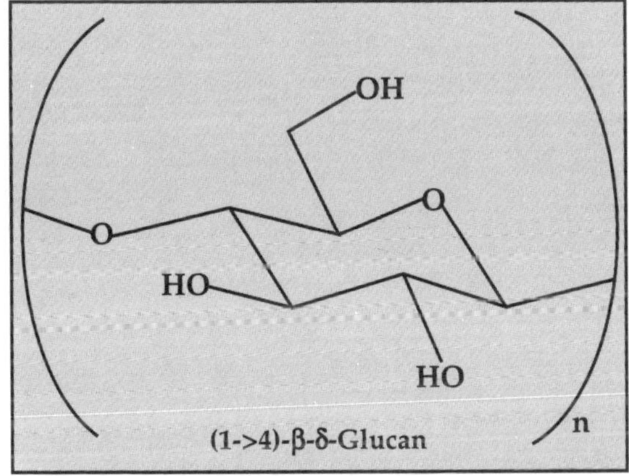

(1->4)-β-δ-Glucan

Fig. 5.5

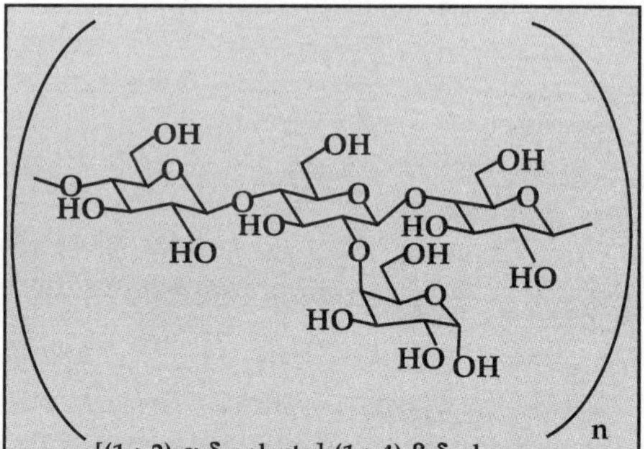

[(1->2)-α-δ-galacto]-(1->4)-β-δ-glucan

Fig. 5.6

A heteropolysaccharide is a polymer containing more than one kind of monosaccharide residue. The parent chain comprised of only one type of monosaccharide, should be listed last with the ending "-an", and the other types of monosaccharides listed in alphabetical order as "glyco-" prefixes. When there is no parent chain, all different monosaccharide residues are to be listed alphabetically as "glyco-" prefixes and the name should end with "-glycan". The following example will help illustrate this concept.

6 Polysaccharide

Polysaccharides are relatively complex carbohydrates. They are polymers made up of many monosaccharides joined together by glycosidic bonds. They are therefore very large, often branched, macromolecules. They tend to be amorphous, insoluble in water, and have no sweet taste.

When all the monosaccharides in a polysaccharide are the same type the polysaccharide is called a *homopolysaccharide*, but when more than one type of monosaccharide is present they are called *heteropolysaccharides*.

Examples include storage polysaccharides such as starch and glycogen and structural polysaccharides such as cellulose and chitin.

Polysaccharides have a general formula of $C_x(H_2O)_y$ where x is usually a large number between 200 and 2500. Considering that the repeating units in the polymer backbone are often six-carbon monosaccharides, the general formula can also be represented as $(C_6H_{10}O_5)_n$ where n={40...3000}.

STORAGE POLYSACCHARIDES

Starches

Starches are glucose polymers in which glucopyranose units are bonded by *alpha*-linkages. It is made up of a mixture of Amylose (15-20%) and Amylopectin (80-85%). Amylose consists of a linear chain of several hundred glucose molecules and Amylopectin is a branched molecule made of several thousand glucose units (every chain 24-30 glucose unit).

Starches are insoluble in water. They can be digested by hydrolysis, catalyzed by enzymes called amylases, which can break the *alpha*-linkages (glycosidic bonds). Humans and other animals have amylases, so they can digest starches. Potato, rice, wheat, and maize are major sources of starch in the human diet. The formation of starches are the way that plants store glucose.

Glycogen

Glycogen is a polysaccharide that is found in animals and is composed of a branched chain of glucose residues. It is stored in liver and muscles.

STRUCTURAL POLYSACCHARIDES

Cellulose

The structural component of plants are formed primarily from cellulose. Wood is largely cellulose and lignin, while paper and cotton are nearly pure cellulose. Cellulose is a polymer made with repeated glucose units bonded together by *beta*-linkages. Humans and many other animals lack an enzyme to break the *beta*-linkages, so they do not digest cellulose. Certain animals can digest cellulose, because bacteria possessing the enzyme are present in their gut. The classic example is the termite.

Acidic Polysaccharides

Acidic polysaccharides are polysaccharides that contain carboxyl groups, phosphate groups and/or sulfuric ester groups.

Bacterial Polysaccharides

Bacterial polysaccharides represent a diverse range of macromolecules that include peptidoglycan, lipopolysaccharides, capsules and exopolysaccharides; compounds whose functions range from structural cell-wall components (eg peptidoglycan), and important virulence factors (e.g. Poly-N-acetylglucosamine in S. aureus), to permitting the bacterium to survive in harsh environments (e.g Pseudomonas aeruginosa in the human lung). Polysaccharide biosynthesis is a tightly regulated, energy intensive process and understanding the subtle interplay between the regulation and energy conservation, polymer modification and synthesis, and the external ecological functions is a huge area of research. The potential benefits are enormous and should enable for example the development of novel antibacterial strategies (e.g. new antibiotics and vaccines) and the commercial exploitation to develop novel applications.

Bacterial Capsule Polysaccharides

Pathogenic bacteria commonly produce a thick, mucous-like, layer of polysaccharide. This "capsule" cloaks antigenic proteins on the bacterial surface that would otherwise provoke an immune response and thereby lead to the destruction of the bacteria. Capsular polysaccharides are water soluble, commonly acidic, and have molecular weights on the order of 100-1000 kDa. They are linear and consist of regularly repeating subunits of one ~ six monosaccharides. There is enormous structural diversity; nearly two hundred different polysaccharides are produced by *E. coli* alone. Mixtures of capsular polysaccharides, either conjugated or native are used as vaccines.

Bacteria and many other microbes, including fungi and algae, often secrete polysaccharides as an evolutionary adaptation to help them adhere to surfaces and to prevent them from drying out. Humans have developed some of these polysaccharides into useful products, including xanthan gum, dextran, gellan gum, and pullulan.

Cell-surface polysaccharides play diverse roles in bacterial ecology and physiology. They serve as a barrier between the cell wall and the environment, mediate host-pathogen interactions, and form structural components of biofilms. These polysaccharides are synthesized from nucleotide-activated precursors (called nucleotide sugars) and, in most cases, all the enzymes necessary for biosynthesis, assembly and transport of the completed polymer are encoded by genes organized in dedicated clusters within the genome of the organism. Lipopolysaccharide is one of the most important cell-surface polysaccharides, as it plays a key structural role in outer membrane integrity, as well as being an important mediator of host-pathogen interactions.

The enzymes that make the *A-band* (homopolymeric) and *B-band* (heteropolymeric) O-antigens have been identified and the metabolic pathways defined The exopolysaccharide alginate is a linear copolymer of ß-1, 4-linked D-mannuronic acid and l-guluronic acid residues, and is responsible for the mucoid phenotype of late-stage cystic fibrosis disease. The *pel* and *psl* loci are two recently discovered gene clusters that also encode exopolysaccharides found to be important for biofilm formation. Rhamnolipid is a biosurfactant whose production is tightly regulated at the transcriptional level, but the precise role that it plays in disease is not well understood at present. Protein glycosylation, particularly of pilin and flagellin, is a recent focus of research by several groups and it has been shown to be important for adhesion and invasion during bacterial infection.

Glycogen

Glycogen is a polysaccharide of glucose (Glc) which functions as the secondary short term energy storage in animal cells. It is made primarily by the liver and the muscles, but can also be made by the brain and stomach Glycogen is the analogue of starch, a less branched glucose polymer in plants, and is commonly referred to as animal starch, having a similar structure to amylopectin. Glycogen is found in the form of granules in the cytosol in many cell types, and plays an important role in the glucose cycle. Glycogen forms an energy reserve that can be quickly mobilized to meet a sudden need for glucose, but one that is less compact than the energy reserves of triglycerides (fat). In the liver hepatocytes, glycogen can compose up to 8% of the fresh weight (100–120 g in an adult) soon after a meal. Only the glycogen stored in the liver can be made accessible to other organs. In the muscles, glycogen is found in a much lower concentration (1% to 2% of the muscle mass), but the total amount exceeds that in liver. However the amount of glycogen in the blood and muscles depends on physical training. Small amounts of glycogen are found in the kidneys, and even smaller amounts in certain glial cells in the brain and white blood cells. The uterus also stores glycogen during pregnancy to nourish the embryo.

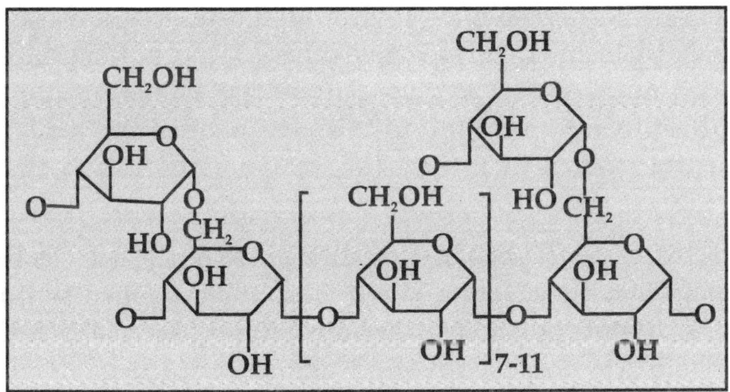

Fig. 6.1

Structure and Biochemistry

Glycogen is a highly branched polymer that is better described as a dendrimer of about 60,000 glucose residues and has a molecular weight between 106 and 107 daltons (~4.8 million). Most of glucose units are linked by a-1,4 glycosidic bonds, approximately 1 in 12 Glc residues also makes alpha-1, 6 glycosidic bond with a second Glc, which results in the creation of a branch. Glycogen does not possess a reducing end: the 'reducing end' glucose residue is not free but is covalently bound to a protein termed glycogenin as a beta-linkage to a surface tyrosine residue. Glycogenin is a glycosyltransferase and occurs as a dimer in the core of glycogen. The glycogen granules contain both glycogen and the enzymes of glycogen synthesis (glycogenesis) and degradation (glycogenolysis). The enzymes are nested between the outer branches of the glycogen molecules and act on the non-reducing ends. Therefore, the many non-reducing end-branches of glycogen facilitate its rapid synthesis and catabolism.

Function and regulation of liver gly al containing carbohydrates is eaten and digested, blood glucose levels rise, and the pancreas secretes insulin. Glucose from the hepatic portal vein enters the liver cells (hepatocytes). Insulin acts on the hepatocytes to stimulate the action of several enzymes, including glycogen synthase. Glucose molecules are added to the chains of glycogen as long as both insulin and glucose remain plentiful. In this postprandial or "fed" state, the liver takes in more glucose from the blood than it releases.

After a meal has been digested and glucose levels begin to fall, insulin secretion is reduced, and glycogen synthesis stops. About four hours after a meal, glycogen begins to be broken down and converted again to glucose. Glycogen phosphorylase is the primary enzyme of glycogen breakdown. For the next 8-12 hours, glucose derived from liver glycogen will be the primary source of blood glucose to be used by the rest of the body for fuel.

Glucagon is another hormone produced by the pancreas, which in many respects serves as a counter-signal to insulin. When the blood sugar begins to fall below normal, glucagon is secreted in increasing amounts. It stimulates glycogen breakdown into glucose even when insulin levels are abnormally high.

In Muscle and Other Cells

Muscle cell glycogen appears to function as an immediate reserve source of available glucose for muscle cells. Other cells that contain small amounts use it locally as well. Muscle cells lack glucose-6-phosphatase enzyme, so they lack the ability to pass glucose into the blood, so the glycogen they store internally is destined for internal use and is not shared with other cells, unlike liver cells.

Glycogen Debt and Endurance Exercise

Due to the body's inability to hold more than around 2,000 kcal of glycogen long-distance athletes such as marathon runners, cross-country skiers, and cyclists go into glycogen debt, where almost all of the athlete's glycogen stores are depleted after long periods of exertion without enough energy consumption. This phenomenon is referred to as "hitting the wall". In marathon runners it normally happens around the 20 mile (32 km) point of a marathon, where around 100 kcal are spent per mile depending on the size of the runner and the race course. However, it can be delayed by a carbohydrate loading before the task.

When experiencing glycogen debt, athletes often experience extreme fatigue to the point that it is difficult to move.

A study published in the *Journal of Applied Physiology* suggests that when athletes ingest both carbohydrate and caffeine following exhaustive exercise, their glycogen is replenished more rapidly.

Disorders of Glycogen Metabolism

The most common disease in which glycogen metabolism becomes abnormal is diabetes, in which, because of abnormal amounts of insulin, liver glycogen can be abnormally accumulated or depleted. Restoration of normal glucose metabolism usually normalizes glycogen metabolism as well.

In hypoglycemia caused by excessive insulin, liver glycogen levels are high, but the high insulin level prevents the glycogenolysis necessary to maintain normal blood sugar levels. Glucagon is a common treatment for this type of hypoglycemia.

Various inborn errors of metabolism are caused by deficiencies of enzymes necessary for glycogen synthesis or breakdown. These are collectively referred to as glycogen storage diseases.

Synthesis

Glycogen synthesis differs from glycogen breakdown. Unlike breakdown, synthesis is endergonic, meaning that glycogen is not synthesized without the input of energy. Energy for glycogen synthesis comes from UTP, which reacts with glucose-1-phosphate, forming UDP-glucose, in reaction catalysed by UDP-glucose pyrophosphorylase. Glycogen is synthesized from monomers of UDP-glucose by the enzyme glycogen synthase, which progressively lengthens the glycogen chain. As glycogen synthase can only lengthen an existing chain, the protein glycogenin is needed to initiate the synthesis of glycogen.

Breakdown

Glycogen is cleaved from the nonreducing ends of the chain by the enzyme glycogen phosphorylase to produce monomers of glucose-1-phosphate that is then converted to glucose 6-phosphate. A special debranching enzyme is needed to remove the alpha(1-6) branches in branched glycogen and reshape the chain into linear polymer. The G6P monomers produced have three possible fates:

- G6P can continue on the glycolysis pathway and be used as fuel.
- G6P can enter the pentose phosphate pathway via the enzyme Glucose-6-phosphate dehydrogenase to produce NADPH and 5-carbon sugars.
- In the liver and kidney, G6P can be dephosphorylated back to Glucose by the enzyme Glucose 6-phosphatase. This is the final step in the gluconeogenesis pathway.

Lactose

Lactose (also referred to as milk sugar) is a sugar that is found most notably in milk. Lactose makes up around 2–8% of milk (by weight). The name comes from the Latin word for milk, plus the -ose ending used to name sugars. Its systematic name is ß-D-galactopyranosyl-(1→4)ß-D-glucopyranose.

Chemistry

Lactose is a disaccharide that consists of ß-δ-galactose and ß-δ-glucose fragments bonded through a ß1-4 glycosidic linkage. As it gives free radicals by mechanochemistry, it is possible to use lactose to follow by ESR (Electron Spin Resonance) the energy used during a milling process.

Solubility

Lactose has a solubility of 1 in 4.63 measured %w/v. This translates to 0.216 g of lactose dissolving readily in 1 mL of water.

The solubility of lactose in water is 18.9049 g at 25°C, 25.1484 g at 40°C and 37.2149 g at 60°C per 100 g solution. Its solubility in ethanol is 0.0111 g at 40°C and 0.0270 g at 60°C per 100 g solution.

Digestion of Lactose (Catabolism)

Infant mammals are fed on milk by their mothers, which is rich in the carbohydrate Lactose. To digest it, an enzyme called lactase (ß-δ-galactosidase) is secreted by the intestinal villi. This enzyme cleaves the lactose molecule into its two subunits; glucose and galactose for absorption.

Since lactose occurs mostly in milk, in most mammals the production of lactase gradually decreases with maturity due to a lack of constant consumption.

Many people who live in Europe, the Middle East, India, and parts of East Africa maintain normal lactase production into adulthood. In many of these areas, milk from mammals such as cattle, goats, and sheep is used as a large source of food. Hence, it was in these regions that genes for lifelong lactase production first evolved. The genes of lactose tolerance have evolved independently in various ethnic groups.

People who are not lactose tolerant may suffer uncomfortable and/or socially unacceptable symptoms of too much lactose consumption. In these people, lactose is not broken down and provides food for gas-producing gut flora. This can lead to bloating, flatulence, and other gastrointestinal symptoms.

Lactose Intolerance

Lactose intolerance is the inability to metabolize lactose, a sugar found in milk and other dairy products, because the required enzyme lactase is absent in the intestinal system or its availability is lowered. It is estimated that 75% of adults worldwide show some decrease in lactase activity during adulthood The frequency of decreased lactase activity ranges from nearly 5% in northern Europe, up to 71% for Southern Europe, to more than 90% in some African and Asian countries.

Overview

Disaccharides cannot be absorbed through the wall of the small intestine into the bloodstream, so in the absence of lactase, lactose present in ingested dairy products remains uncleaved and passes intact into the colon. The operons of enteric bacteria quickly switch over to lactose metabolism, and the resultant in vivo fermentation produces copious amounts of gas (a mixture of hydrogen, carbon dioxide, and methane). This, in turn, may cause a range of abdominal symptoms, including stomach cramps, bloating, and flatulence. In addition, as with other unabsorbed sugars (such as sorbitol, mannitol, and xylitol), the presence of lactose and its fermentation products raises the osmotic pressure of the colon contents.

Classification

There are three major types of lactose intolerance:

- **Primary lactose intolerance**. Environmentally induced when weaning a child in non-dairy consuming societies. This is found in many Asian and African cultures, where industrialized and commercial dairy products are uncommon.
- **Secondary lactose intolerance**. Environmentally induced, resulting from certain gastrointestinal diseases, including exposure to intestinal parasites such as giardia. In such cases the production of lactase may be permanently disrupted A very common cause of temporary lactose intolerance is gastroenteritis, particularly when the gastroenteritis is caused by rotavirus. Another form of temporary lactose intolerance is lactose overload in infants.
- **Congenital lactase deficiency**. A genetic disorder which prevents enzymatic production of lactase. Present at birth, and diagnosed in early infancy.

Lactase Biology

The normal mammalian condition is for the young of a species to experience reduced lactase production at the end of the weaning period (a species-specific length of time). In non dairy consuming societies, lactase production usually drops about 90% during the first four years of life, although the exact drop over time varies widely.

However, certain human populations have a mutation on chromosome 2 which eliminates the shutdown in lactase production, making it possible for members of these populations to continue consumption of fresh milk and other dairy products throughout their lives without difficulty. This appears to be an evolutionarily recent adaptation to dairy consumption, and has occurred independently in both northern Europe and east Africa in populations with a historically pastoral lifestyle. Lactase persistence, allowing lactose digestion to continue into adulthood, is a dominant allele, making lactose intolerance a recessive genetic trait.

Some cultures, such as that of Japan, where dairy consumption has been on the increase, demonstrate a lower prevalence of lactose intolerance in spite of a genetic predisposition.

Pathological lactose intolerance can be caused by Coeliac disease, which damages the villi in the small intestine that produce lactase. This lactose intolerance is temporary. Lactose intolerance associated with coeliac disease ceases after the patient has been on a gluten-free diet long enough for the villi to recover.

Certain people who report problems with consuming lactose are not actually lactose intolerant. In a study of 323 Sicilian adults, found only 4% were both lactose intolerant and lactose maldigesters, while 32.2% were lactose maldigesters but did not test as lactose intolerant. However, researchers found that 72% of 100 Sicilians were lactose intolerant in their study and 106 of 208 northern Italians (i.e., 51%) were lactose intolerant.

Lactose intolerance levels also increase with age. At ages 2-3 years, 6 year, and 9-10 years, the amount of lactose intolerance is, respectively:

- 6% to 15% in white Americans and northern Europeans.
- 18%, 30%, and 47% in Mexican Americans.
- 25%, 45%, and 60% in black South Africans.
- approximately 10%, 20%, and 25% in Chinese and Japanese.
- 30-55%, 90%, and >90% in Mestizos of Peru.

Chinese and Japanese populations typically lose between 20 and 30 per cent of their ability to digest lactose within three to four years of weaning. Some studies have found that most Japanese can consume 200 ml (8 fl oz) of milk without severe symptoms.

Ashkenazi Jews can keep 20-30 per cent of their ability to digest lactose for many years of the 10% of the Northern European population that develops lactose intolerance, the development of lactose intolerance is a gradual process spread out over as many as 20 years.

Diagnosis

To assess lactose intolerance, the intestinal function is challenged by ingesting more dairy than can be readily digested. Clinical symptoms typically appear within 30 minutes but may take up to 1-2 hours depending on other foods and activities. Substantial variability of the clinical response (symptoms of nausea, cramping, bloating, diarrhea, and flatulence) are to be expected as the extent and severity of lactose intolerance varies between individuals.

When considering the need for confirmation, it is important to distinguish lactose intolerance from milk allergy, which is an abnormal immune response (usually) to milk proteins. Since lactose intolerance is the normal state for most adults on a worldwide scale, and not considered a disease condition, a medical diagnosis is not normally required. However, if confirmation is necessary, three tests are available.

Hydrogen Breath Test

In a hydrogen breath test, after an overnight fast, 50 grams of lactose (in a solution with water) is swallowed. If the lactose cannot be digested, enteric bacteria metabolize it and produce hydrogen. This, along with methane, can be detected in the patient's breath by a clinical gas chromatograph or a compact solid state detector. The test takes about 2 to 3 hours. A medical condition with similar symptoms is fructose malabsorption.

In conjunction, measuring the blood glucose level every 10-15 minutes after ingestion will show a "flat curve" in individuals with lactose malabsorption, while the lactase persistent will have a significant "top", with an elevation of typically 50 to 100% within 1-2 hours. However, given the need for frequent blood drawns, this approach has been largely supplanted by breath testing.

Stool Acidity

Can be used to diagnose lactose intolerance in small infants, for whom other forms of testing are risky or impractical.

Intestinal Biopsy

An intestinal biopsy can confirm lactose intolerance following discovery of elevated hydrogen in the hydrogen breath test. However, given the invasive nature of this test, and the need for a highly specialized laboratory to measure lactase enzymes or mRNA in the biopsy tissue, this approach is used almost exclusively in clinical research.

History of Diagnosis

The ancient Greek physician Hippocrates (460-370 B.C.) first noted gastrointestinal upset and skin problems in some who consumed milk patients experiencing the former symptom may likely have been suffering from lactose intolerance. However, it was only in the last few decades that the syndrome was more widely described by modern medical science.

The condition was first recognized in the 1950s and 1960s when various organizations like the United Nations began to engage in systematic famine-relief efforts in countries outside Europe for the first time. Holzel *et al.* (1959)

and Durand (1959) produced two of the earliest studies of lactose intolerance. As anecdotes of embarrassing dairy-induced discomfort increased, the First World donor countries could no longer ascribe the reports to spoilage in transit or inappropriate food preparation by the Third World recipients.

Because the first nations to industrialize and develop modern scientific medicine were dominated by people of European descent, adult dairy consumption was long taken for granted. Westerners for some time did not recognize that the majority of the human ethno-genetic groups could not consume dairy products during adulthood. Although there had been regular contact between Europeans and non-Europeans throughout history, the notion that large-scale medical studies should be representative of the ethnic diversity of the human populations (as well as all genders and ages) did not become well-established until after the American Civil Rights Movement.

Since then, the relationship between lactase and lactose has been thoroughly investigated in food science due to the growing market for dairy products among non-Europeans.

Originally it was hypothesised that gut bacteria such as *E. coli* produced the lactase enzyme needed to cleave lactose into its constituent monosaccharides and thus become metabolisable and digestible by humans. Some form of human-bacteria symbiosis was proposed as a means of producing lactase in the human digestive tract. Genetics and protein analysis techniques by the early 1970s revealed this to be untrue; humans produce their own lactase enzyme natively in intestine cells.

According to Heyman (2006), approximately 70% of the global population cannot tolerate lactose in adulthood. Thus, some argue that the terminology should be reversed — lactose intolerance should be seen as the norm, and the minority groups should be labeled as having *lactase persistence*.

A counter argument to this is that the cultures that don't generally consume unmodified milk products have little need to discuss their intolerance to it, leaving the cultures for which lactose intolerance is a significant dietary issue to define its terminology.

History of Genetic Prevalence

Lactose intolerance has been studied as an aid in understanding ancient diets and population movement in prehistoric societies. Milking an animal vastly increases the calories that may be extracted from the animal as compared to the consumption of its meat alone. It is not surprising then, that consuming milk products became an important part of the agricultural way of life in the Neolithic. It is believed that most of the milk was used to make mature cheeses which are mostly lactose free.

Roman authors recorded that the people of northern Europe, particularly Britain and Germany drank unprocessed milk (as opposed to the Romans who made cheese). This corresponds very closely with modern European distributions of lactose intolerance, where the people of Britain, Germany and Scandinavia have a good tolerance, and those of southern Europe, especially Italy, have a poorer tolerance.

In east Asia, historical sources also attest that the Chinese did not consume milk, whereas the nomads that lived on the borders did. Again, this reflects modern distributions of intolerance. China is particularly notable as a place of poor tolerance, whereas in Mongolia and the Asian steppes horse milk is drunk regularly. This tolerance is thought to be advantageous as the nomads do not settle down long enough to process mature cheese. Given that their prime source of income is generated through horses, to ignore their milk as a source of calories would be greatly detrimental. The nomads also make an alcoholic beverage, called Kumis, from horse milk, although the fermentation process reduces the amount of lactose present.

The African Fulani have a nomadic origin and their culture once completely revolved around cow, goat, and sheep herding. Dairy products were once a large source of nutrition for them. As might be expected if lactase persistence evolved in response to dairy product consumption, they are particularly tolerant to lactose (about 77% of the population). Many Fulani live in Guinea-Conakry, Burkina Faso, Mali, Nigeria, Niger, Cameroon, and Chad.

There is some debate on exactly where and when genetic mutation(s) occurred. Some argue for separate mutation events in Sweden (which has one of the lowest levels of lactose intolerance in the world) and the Arabian Peninsula around 4000 BC. However, others argue for a single mutation event in the Middle East at about 4500 BC which then subsequently radiated. Some sources suggest a third and more recent mutation in the East African Tutsi. Whatever the precise origin in time and place, most modern Northern Europeans and people of European ancestry show the effects of this mutation (that is, they are able to safely consume milk products all their lives) while most modern East Asians, sub-Saharan Africans and native peoples of the Americas and Pacific Islands do not (making them lactose intolerant as adults). The Maasai ability to consume dairy without exhibiting symptoms may be due to a different genetic mutation. Or it may be due to the fact that they curdle their milk before they consume it, removing the lactose.

A noncoding variation in the MCM6 gene has been strongly associated with adult type hypolactasia.

Managing Lactose Intolerance

For persons living in societies where the diet contains relatively little dairy, lactose intolerance is not considered a condition that requires treatment. However, those living among societies that are largely lactose-tolerant may find lactose intolerance troublesome. Although there are still no methodologies to reinstate lactase production, some individuals have reported their intolerance to vary over time (depending on health status and pregnancy. Lactose intolerance is not usually an all-or-nothing condition: the reduction in lactase production, and hence, the amount of lactose that can be tolerated varies from person to person. Since lactose intolerance poses no further threat to a person's health, managing the condition consists of minimizing the occurrence and severity of symptoms. Berdanier and Hargrove recognise four general principles:

1. avoidance of dietary lactose;
2. substitution to maintain nutrient intake;
3. regulation of calcium intake; and
4. use of enzyme substitute.

Avoiding Lactose-containing Products

Since each individual's tolerance to lactose varies, according to the US National Institute of Health, "Dietary control of lactose intolerance depends on people learning through trial and error how much lactose they can handle." Label reading is essential as commercial terminology varies according to language and region.

Lactose is present in two large food categories: Conventional dairy products, and as a food additive (in dairy and non-dairy products).

Dairy Products

Lactose is a water-soluble molecule. Therefore fat percentage and the curdling process have an impact on which foods may be tolerated. In the curdling process lactose is found in the water portion along with whey and casein, but is not found in the fat portion. Dairy products which are "fat reduced" or "fat free" generally have a slightly higher lactose percentage. Additionally, low fat dairy foods also often have various dairy derivatives such as milk solids added to them to enhance sweetness, increasing the lactose content.

Milk

Human milk has the highest lactose percentage at around nine per cent. Unprocessed cow milk has 4.7% lactose. Unprocessed milk from other bovids contains similar lactose percentages (goat milk 4.1% buffalo 4.86%, yak 4.93%, sheep milk 4.6%).

Butter

The butter-making process separates the majority of milk's water components from the fat components. Lactose, being a water soluble molecule, will be present in small quantities in the butter unless it is also fermented to produce cultured butter.

Yogurt and Kefir

People can be more tolerant of traditionally made yogurt than milk because it contains lactase enzyme produced by the bacterial cultures used to make the yogurt. However, many commercial brands contain milk solids, increasing the lactose content.

Cheeses

Traditionally made hard cheese (such as Swiss cheese) and soft ripened cheeses may create less reaction than the equivalent amount of milk because of the processes involved. Fermentation and higher fat content contribute to lesser amounts of lactose. Traditionally made Swiss or Cheddar might contain 10% of the lactose found in whole milk. In addition, the traditional aging methods of cheese (over two years) reduces their lactose content to practically nothing Commercial cheese brands, however, are generally manufactured by modern processes that do not have the same lactose reducing properties, and as no regulations mandate what qualifies as an "aged" cheese, this description does not provide any indication of whether the process used significantly reduced lactose.

Sour Cream and Ice-cream

Like yogurt, if made the traditional way, may be tolerable, but most modern brands add milk solids. Consult labels.

Examples of Lactose Levels in Foods

As scientific consensus has not been reached concerning lactose percentage analysis methods non-hydrated form or the mono-hydrated form), and considering that dairy content varies greatly according to labelling practices, geography and manufacturing processes, lactose numbers may not be very reliable. The following are examples of lactose levels in foods which commonly set off symptoms. These quantities are to be treated as guidelines only.

Dairy Product	Lactose Content
Yogurt, plain, low-fat, 240 mL	5g
Milk, reduced fat, 240 mL	11g
Swiss cheese, 28g	1g
Ice cream, 120 mL	6 g
Cottage cheese, 120 mL	2-3 g

Lactose in Non-dairy Products

Lactose (also present when labels state lactoserum, whey, milk solids, modified milk ingredients, etc.) is a commercial food additive used for its texture, flavor and adhesive qualities, and is found in foods such as processed meats (sausages/hot dogs, sliced meats, Pâtés), gravy stock powder, margarines sliced breads, breakfast cereals, potato chips, dried fruit, processed foods, medications, prepared meals, meal replacement (powders and bars), protein supplements (powders and bars)

Kosher products labelled *parevc* are free of milk. However, if a "D" (for "Dairy) is present next to the circled

"K", "U", or other hechsher, the food likely contains milk solids (although it may also simply indicate that the product was produced on equipment shared with other products containing milk derivatives).

Alternative Products

Plant based milks and derivatives are the only ones to be 100% lactose free: soy milk, rice milk, almond milk, hazelnut milk, oat milk, hemp milk, peanut milk, horchata.

The dairy industry has created low-lactose or lactose-free products to replace regular dairy. Lactose-free milk can be produced by passing milk over lactase enzyme bound to an inert carrier: once the molecule is cleaved, there are no lactose ill-effects. A form is available with reduced amounts of lactose (typically 30% of normal), and alternatively with nearly 0%. Finland, where approximately 17% of the Finnish-speaking population has hypolactasia, has had "HYLA" (acronym for *hydrolysed lactose*) products available for many years. These low-lactose level cow's milk products, ranging from ice cream to cheese, use a Valio patented chromatographic separation method to remove lactose. The ultra-pasteurization process, combined with aseptic packaging, ensures a long shelf-life. Recently, the range of low-lactose products available in Finland has been augmented with milk and other dairy products (such as ice cream, butter, and buttermilk) that contain no lactose at all. The remaining about 20% of lactose in HYLA products is taken care of enzymatically. These typically cost slightly more than equivalent products containing lactose. Valio also markets these products in Sweden and in Estonia.

Alternatively, a bacterium such as *L. acidophilus* may be added, which affects the lactose in milk the same way it affects the lactose in yogurt.

Lactase Supplementation

When lactose avoidance is not possible, or on occasions when a person chooses to consume such items, then enzymatic lactase supplements may be used.

Lactase enzymes similar to those produced in the small intestines of humans are produced industrially by fungi of the genus *aspergillus*. The enzyme, ß-galactosidase, is available in tablet form in a variety of doses, in many countries without a prescription. It functions well only in high-acid environments, such as that found in the human gut due to the addition of gastric juices from the stomach. Unfortunately, too much acid can denature it and it, therefore, should not be taken on an empty stomach. Also, the enzyme is ineffective if it does not reach the small intestine by the time the problematic food does. Lactose-sensitive individuals should experiment with both timing and dosage to fit their particular need. But supplements such as these may not be able to provide the accurate amount of lactase needed to adequately digest the lactose contained in dairy products, which may lead to symptoms similar to the existing lactose intolerance.

While essentially the same process as normal intestinal lactose digestion, direct treatment of milk employs a different variety of industrially produced lactase. This enzyme, produced by yeast from the genus *kluyveromyces*, takes much longer to act, must be thoroughly mixed throughout the product, and is destroyed by even mildly acidic environments. It therefore has been much less popular as a consumer product (sold, where available, as a liquid) than the *aspergillus*-produced tablets, despite its predictable effectiveness. Its main use is in producing the lactose-free or lactose-reduced dairy products sold in supermarkets

Enzymatic lactase supplementation may have an advantage over avoiding dairy products, in that alternative provision does not need to be made to provide sufficient calcium intake, especially in children.

Rehabituation to Dairy Products

For healthy individuals with secondary lactose intolerance, it may be possible to train bacteria in the large intestine to break down lactose more effectively by consuming small quantities of dairy products several times a day over a couple of weeks. Reintroducing dairy in this way to people who have an underlying or chronic illness, however, is not recommended, as certain illnesses damage the intestinal tract in a way which prevents the lactase enzyme from being expressed.

Some studies indicate that environmental factors (more specifically, the consumption of lactose) may "play a more important role than genetic factors in the etio-pathogenesis of milk intolerance" but some other publications suggest that lactase production does not seem to be induced by dairy/ lactose consumption.

NUTRITIONAL CONCERNS

Primary Lactose Intolerance

Populations where primary lactose intolerance is the norm have demonstrated similar health levels to westerners (outside of malnutrition issues; see the History of genetic prevalence subsection above) or better health (Japan).

Secondary Lactose Intolerance

While secondary lactose intolerance does not inherently affect an individual's nutritional needs, according to accepted medical doctrines in western European and North American countries, dairy is an essential part of a healthy diet. Dairy products are relatively good and accessible sources of calcium and potassium and many countries mandate that milk be fortified with vitamin A and vitamin D. Consequently, in dairy-consuming societies, dairy is often a main source of these nutrients; and, for lacto-vegetarians, a main source of vitamin B_{12}. Individuals who reduce or eliminate consumption of dairy must obtain these nutrients elsewhere. However, Asian populations for whom dairy is not part of their food culture do not present decreased health and sometimes present above average health, like in Japan.

Plant based milk substitutes are not naturally rich in calcium, potassium, or vitamins A or D (and, like most non-animal products, contain no vitamin B_{12}). However, prominent brands are often voluntarily fortified with many of these nutrients.

An increasing number of calcium-fortified breakfast foods, such as orange juice, bread, and dry cereal have been appearing on supermarket shelves. Many fruits and vegetables are rich in potassium and vitamin A; animal products like meat and eggs are rich in vitamin B_{12}, and the human body itself produces some vitamin D from exposure to direct sunlight. Finally, a dietitian or physician may recommend a vitamin or mineral supplement to make up for any remaining nutritional shortfall.

Lactose-reduced dairy products have the same nutritional content as their full-lactose counterparts, but their taste and appearance may differ slightly.

Most infants with gastroenteritis due to rotavirus do not develop lactose intolerance so these infants do not benefit from being put on a lactose-free diet unless symptoms of lactose intolerance are severe and persistent.

Congenital Lactase Deficiency

Congenital lactase deficiency, or CLD, is an autosomal recessive disorder which prevents the expression of lactase. Before the 20th century, infants with this disease rarely survived. As substitute and lactose-free infant formulas later became available, nursing infants affected with CLD could now have their normal nutritional needs met. Beyond infancy, individuals with CLD usually have the same nutritional concerns as those affected by secondary lactose intolerance.

Fructose Malabsorption

Fructose malabsorption, formerly inappropriately named "dietary fructose intolerance", is a digestive disorder of the small intestine in which the fructose carrier in enterocytes is deficient. This problem results in the concentration of fructose in the entire intestine to be increased. Fructose malabsorption is found in approximately 30-40% of the population of Central Europe, with about half of the affected individuals exhibiting symptoms.

Fructose Malabsorption is not to be confused with Hereditary Fructose Intolerance (HFI), a condition in which the liver enzymes that break up fructose are deficient.

Diagnosis

Medical tests are similar as in lactose intolerance, requiring a hydrogen breath test for a clinical diagnosis. When breath test cannot be done from some reason, reducing substances in the stool, and subsequently fructose in the stool can be checked.

It can be associated with reduced plasma tryptophan and clinical depression.

Pathophysiology

Fructose is absorbed in the small intestine without help of digestive enzymes. However, even in healthy people, only about 25-50 g of fructose per sitting can be absorbed. Persons with fructose malabsorption may absorb less then 25 g per sitting (amount is arbitrary determined according to investigation of fructose absorption is many individuals) In the large intestine the unabsorbed fructose osmotically reduces the absorption of water and is metabolized by normal colonic bacteria to short chain fatty acids and the gases hydrogen, carbon dioxide and methane. The abnormal increase in hydrogen is detected with the hydrogen breath test.

The physiological consequences of fructose malabsorption include increasing osmotic load, providing substrate for rapid bacterial fermentation, changing gastrointestinal motility, promoting mucosal biofilm and altering the profile of bacteria. These effects are additive with other short-chain poorly absorbed carbohydrates such as sorbitol. The clinical significance of these events depends upon the response of the bowel to such changes; they have a higher chance of inducing symptoms in patients with functional gut disorders than asymptomatic subjects. Some effects of fructose malabsorption are decreased tryptophan, folic acid and zinc in the blood Restricting dietary intake of free fructose and/or fructans may have durable symptomatic benefits in a high proportion of patients with functional gut disorders, but high quality evidence is lacking.

Treatment

There is no known cure, but an appropriate diet will help.

Diet

Principle of diet in frucose malabsorption is in avoiding:

- Fructose-rich foods or any fructose-containing food in large amount.
- Foods with high fructose-to-glucose ratio (Glucose enhances absorption of fructose, so fructose from foods with fructose-to-glucose ratio <1, like bananas) are readilly absorbed, while foods with fructose-to-glucose ratio >1 (like apples and pears) are often problematic, regardless of actual amount of fructose in the food).
- Foods with high fructose corn syrup (HFCS).
- Foods rich in sorbitol.
- Foods rich in fructans or other FODMAPs (problematic only in some persons with FM).

Depending upon the sufferer's sensitivity to fructose, small amounts of problem foods could be eaten (especially when they are not the main ingredient of a meal).

Foods with a high glucose content actually help sufferers absorb fructose.

Symptoms

This condition is common in patients with symptoms of Irritable Bowel Syndrome and most patients with fructose malabsorption fit the profile of those with Irritable Bowel Syndrome A small proportion of patients with both **fructose** malabsorption and lactose intolerance also suffer from celiac disease.

Typical symptoms of fructose malabsorption include:

- Bloating (because of fermentation in the small and large intestine).
- Diarrhoea and/or constipation.
- Flatulence.
- Stomach pain (due to muscle spasms, which can vary from mild and chronic to acute but erratic).

Other possible symptoms of fructose malabsorption include:

- Aching eyes
- Fuzzy head
- Fatigue
- Depression as a result of absorption disorders in the small and large intestines, other substances such as amino acids are not absorbed. Because of missing substances (among others tryptophan), hormones and neurotransmitters cannot be synthesized.

There is a lot of misinformation and misconception about fruit sugar content. A common belief is that fruits contain mainly, or only, fructose sugar. The USDA food database reveals that many common fruits contain nearly equal amounts of the fructose and glucose. There is a tendency within plants to keep these sugars 50/50. Some aberrantly high fructose fruits are apple, pear, and watermelon, which have over twice as much fructose as glucose. Fructose levels in grapes varies with ripeness and variety, with unripe grapes containing more glucose.

Foods with High Fructan Content

Chains of fructose molecules known as fructans occur naturally in many foods. The following foods have a high fructan content:

- Artichokes
- Asparagus
- Leeks
- Onions including spring onion
- Wheat including most beers, breads, cakes, biscuits, breakfast cereals, pies, pastas, pizzas, and some noodles.

The role that fructans play in fructose malabsorption is still under investigation. However, it is recommended that fructan intake for fructose mal-absorber should be kept to less than 0.5 gram/serving and supplements with *inulin* and *fructooligosaccharide* (FOS), fructans, intake should be avoided.

Other Problem Foods

In addition, the following foods can cause symptoms of fructose malabsorption:

- Sodas and other beverages containing high fructose corn syrup (HFCS)
- Dried fruit (including "health" bars containing dried fruit)
- Tinned fruit in "natural" juice (which is often pear juice)
- Sorbitol (present in some diet drinks and foods, and occurring naturally in some stone fruits)
- Xylitol present in some berries, and other polyols (sugar alcohols), such as erythritol, mannitol, and other ingredients that end with -tol, commonly added as artificial sweeteners in commercial foods.

- Sweet wines.
- Too much fruit or any food product containing fructose, sorbitol, HFCS, or polyols in a short time frame.

Dietary Guidelines for the Management of Fructose Malabsorption

Dietary guidelines have been developed for managing fructose malabsorption particularly for individuals with IBS.

Unfavourable Foods (i.e. more fructose than glucose)

- Fruit - apple, pear, guava, honeydew melon, nashi fruit, pawpaw/papaya, quince, star fruit, watermelon.
- Dried fruit - apple, apricot, currant, date, fig, pear, prune, raisin, sultana.
- Fruit juices.
- Fruit pastes - chutney, relish, plum sauce, sweet & sour sauce, BBQ sauce.
- Coconut.
- Dried fruit bars.
- Honey.
- Fortified wines.
- High Fructose Corn Syrup - many processed products contain this.
- Corn syrup solids.
- Fruit juice concentrates.
- Agave syrup.

Favourable Foods (i.e. fructose equal to or less than glucose)

- Stone fruit: apricot, nectarine, peach, plum (caution - these fruit contain sorbitol).

- Berry fruit: blueberry, blackberry, boysenberry, cranberry, raspberry, strawberry.
- Citrus fruit: kumquat, grapefruit, lemon, lime, mandarin, orange, tangelo.
- Other fruits: ripe banana, jackfruit, kiwi fruit, passion fruit, pineapple, rhubarb, tamarillo.

Food Labelling Laws

Producers of processed food are not currently required by law to mark foods containing "fructose in excess of glucose." This can cause some surprises and pitfalls for fructose malabsorbers.

Note that foods (such as bread) marked "gluten-free" are usually suitable for fructose malabsorbers, though sufferers need to be careful of gluten-free foods that contain dried fruit or high fructose corn syrup or fructose itself in sugar form. However, fructose malabsorbers do *not* need to avoid gluten as do those with celiac disease.

Many fructose malabsorbers can eat breads made from rye and corn flour. However, these may contain wheat unless marked "wheat-free" (or "gluten-free") (Note, rye bread is NOT gluten-free). Although often assumed to be an acceptable alternative to wheat, spelt flour is not suitable for sufferers of fructose malabsorption, just as it is not appropriate for those with wheat-allergies or celiac disease (while bread made from spelt *sprouts* may be tolerated by the latter). However, some fructose malabsorbers do not have difficulty with fructans from wheat products while they may have problems with foods that contain excess free fructose.

Note that there are many breads on the market that advertise themselves with phrases like: "No High Fructose Corn Syrup". Many bakeries now produce special breads with a high-inulin content, where inulin is a replacement in the baking process for all three: high fructose corn syrup, flour, and fat. Because of the caloric reduction, lower fat content, dramatic fiber increase, and prebiotic tendencies of the replacement inulin, these breads are considered a healthier alternative to traditionally prepared leavening breads. Inulin breads may even highlight the absence of high fructose corn syrup in the bread. However significant these health advances may be, sufferers of fructose malabsorption will likely find no difference between these new breads and traditionally prepared breads in the areas of flatulence or stool, because inulin is a fructan.

Glucose-galactose Malabsorption

Glucose-galactose malabsorption is a condition in which the cells lining the intestine cannot take in the sugars glucose and galactose, which prevents proper digestion of these molecules and larger molecules made from them.

Glucose and galactose are called simple sugars, or monosaccharides. Sucrose and lactose are called disaccharides because they are made from two simple sugars, and are broken down into these simple sugars during digestion. Sucrose is broken down into glucose and another simple sugar called fructose, and lactose is broken down into glucose and galactose. As a result, lactose, sucrose and other compounds made from carbohydrates cannot be digested by individuals with glucose-galactose malabsorption.

Diagnosis

Glucose-galactose malabsorption generally becomes apparent in the first few weeks of a baby's life. Affected infants experience severe diarrhea resulting in life-threatening dehydration, increased acidity of the blood and tissues (acidosis), and weight loss when fed breast milk or regular infant formulas. However, they are able to digest fructose-based formulas that do not contain glucose or galactose. Some affected children are better able to tolerate glucose and galactose as they get older.

Small amounts of glucose in the urine (mild glucosuria) may occur intermittently in this disorder. Affected individuals may also develop kidney stones or more widespread deposits of calcium within the kidneys.

Glucose-galactose malabsorption is a rare disorder; only a few hundred cases have been identified worldwide. However, as many as 10 percent of the population may have a somewhat reduced capacity for glucose absorption without associated health problems. This condition may be a milder variation of glucose-galactose malabsorption.

Genetics

The *SLC5A1* gene provides instructions for producing a sodium/glucose cotransporter protein called SGLT1. This protein is found mainly in the intestinal tract and, to a lesser extent, in the kidneys, where it is involved in transporting glucose and the structurally similar galactose across cell membranes. The sodium/glucose cotransporter protein is important in the functioning of intestinal epithelial cells, which are cells that line the walls of the intestine. These cells have fingerlike projections called microvilli that absorb nutrients from food as it passes through the intestine. Based on their appearance, groups of these microvilli are known collectively as the brush border. The sodium/glucose cotransporter protein is involved in the process of using energy to move glucose and galactose across the brush border membrane for absorption, a mechanism called active transport. Sodium and water are transported across the brush border along with the sugars in this process.

Mutations that prevent the sodium/glucose cotransporter protein from performing this function result in a buildup of glucose and galactose in the intestinal tract. This failure of active transport prevents the glucose and galactose from being absorbed and providing nourishment to the body. In addition, the water that normally would have been transported across the brush border with the sugar instead remains in the intestinal tract to be expelled with the stool, resulting in dehydration of the body's tissues and severe diarrhea.

This condition is inherited in an autosomal recessive pattern, which means two copies of the gene in each cell are altered. Most often, the parents of an individual with an autosomal recessive disorder each carry one copy of the altered gene but do not show signs and symptoms of the disorder. In some cases, individuals with one altered gene have reduced levels of glucose absorption capacity as measured in laboratory tests, but this has not generally been shown to have significant health effects.

8 Carbohydrate

Carbohydrates (from 'hydrates of carbon') or saccharides are the most abundant of the four major classes of biomolecules. They fill numerous roles in living things, such as the storage and transport of energy (e.g.: starch, glycogen) and structural components (e.g.: cellulose in plants, chitin and cartilage in animals). Additionally, carbohydrates and their derivatives play major roles in the working process of the immune system, fertilization, pathogenesis, blood clotting, and development.

Chemically, carbohydrates are simple organic compounds that are aldehydes or ketones with many hydroxyl groups added, usually one on each carbon atom that is not part of the aldehyde or ketone functional group. The basic carbohydrate units are called monosaccharides, such as glucose, galactose, and fructose. The general stoichiometric formula of an unmodified monosaccharide is $(CH_2O)_n$, where n is any number of three or greater; however, not all carbohydrates conform to this precise stoichiometric definition (e.g.: uronic acids, deoxy-sugars such as fucose), nor are all chemicals that do conform to this definition automatically classified as carbohydrates.

Monosaccharides can be linked together into what are called polysaccharides (or oligosaccharides) in almost limitless ways. Many carbohydrates contain one or more modified monosaccharide units that have had one or more groups replaced or removed. For example, deoxyribose, a component of DNA, is a modified version of ribose; chitin is composed of repeating units of N-acetylglucosamine, a nitrogen-containing form of glucose.

While the scientific nomenclature of carbohydrates is complex, the names of carbohydrates very often end in the suffix - ose.

Monosaccharides

Monosaccharides are the simplest carbohy-drates in that they cannot be hydrolyzed to smaller carbohydrates. The general chemical formula of an unmodified monosa-ccharide is $(CH_2O)_n$, where n is any number of three or greater (*also see ch. 4 on Monosaccharide*).

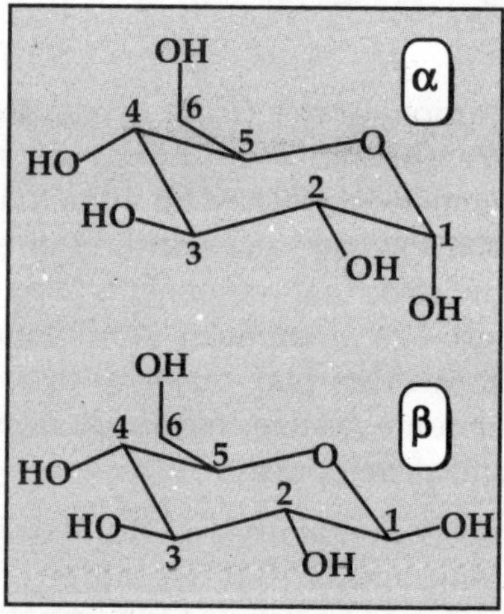

Fig. 8.1: **The α and β anomers of glucose. Note the position of the anomeric carbon (red or green) relative to the CH_2 OH group bound to carbon S: they are either on the opposite sides (α), or the same side (β)**

Classification of Monosaccharides

Monosaccharides are classified according to three different charac-teristics: the placement of its carbonyl group, the number of carbon atoms it contains, and its chiral handedness. If the carbonyl group is an aldehyde, the monosaccharide is an aldose; if the carbonyl group is a ketone, the monosaccharide is a ketose. Monosaccharides with three carbon atoms are called trioses, those with four are called tetroses, five are called pentoses, six are hexoses, and so on. These two systems of classification are often combined. For example, glucose is an aldohexose (a six-carbon aldehyde), ribose is an aldopentose (a five-carbon aldehyde), and fructose is a ketohexose (a six-carbon ketone).

Each carbon atom bearing a hydroxyl group (-OH), with the exception of the first and last carbons, are asymmetric, making them stereocenters with two possible configurations each (R or S). Because of this asymmetry, a number of isomers may exist for any given monosaccharide formula. The aldohexose δ-glucose, for example, has the formula $(CH_2O)_6$, of which all but two of its six carbons atoms are stereogenic, making δ-glucose one of $2^4 = 16$ possible stereoisomers. In the case of glyceraldehyde, an aldotriose, there is one pair of possible stereoisomers, which are enantiomers and epimers. 1, 3-dihydroxyacetone, the ketose corresponding to the aldose glyceraldehyde, is a symmetric molecule with no stereocenters). The assignment of δ or l is made according to the orientation of the asymmetric carbon furthest from the carbonyl group: in a standard Fischer projection if the hydroxyl group is on the right the molecule is a δ sugar, otherwise it is an l sugar. Because δ sugars are biologically far more common, the δ is often omitted.

Conformation

The aldehyde or ketone group of a straight-chain monosaccharide will react reversibly with a hydroxyl group on a different carbon atom to form a hemiacetal or hemiketal, forming a heterocyclic ring with an oxygen bridge between two carbon atoms. Rings with five and six atoms are called furanose and pyranose forms, respectively, and exist in equilibrium with the straight-chain form.

During the conversion from straight-chain form to cyclic form, the carbon atom containing the carbonyl oxygen, called the anomeric carbon, becomes a chiral center with two possible configurations: the oxygen atom may take a position either above or below the plane of the ring. The resulting possible pair of stereoisomers are called anomers. In the *a anomer*, the -OH substituent on the anomeric carbon rests on the opposite side (trans) of the ring from the CH_2OH side branch. The alternative form, in which the CH_2OH substituent and the anomeric hydroxyl are on the same side (cis) of the plane of the ring, is called the *ß anomer*. You can remember that the ß anomer is cis by the mnemonic, "It's always better to ße up". Because the ring and straight-chain forms readily interconvert, both anomers exist in equilibrium.

Use in Living Organisms

Monosaccharides are the major source of fuel for metabolism, being used both as an energy source (glucose being the most important in nature) and in biosynthesis. When monosaccharides are not immediately needed by many cells they are often converted to more space efficient forms, often polysaccharides. In many animals, including humans, this storage form is glycogen, especially in liver and muscle cells. In plants, starch is used for the same purpose.

Disaccharides

Two joined monosaccharides are called a disaccharide and these are the simplest polysaccharides. Examples include sucrose and lactose. They are composed of two monosaccharide units bound together by a covalent bond known as a glycosidic linkage formed via a dehydration reaction, resulting in the loss of a hydrogen atom from one monosaccharide and a hydroxyl group from the other. The formula of unmodified disaccharides is $C_{12}H_{22}O_{11}$. Although there are numerous kinds of disaccharides, a handful of disaccharides are particularly notable.

Sucrose, pictured to the right, is the most abundant disaccharide, and the main form in which carbohydrates are transported in plants. It is composed of one δ-glucose molecule and one δ-fructose molecule. The systematic name for sucrose, *O*-a-δ-glucopyranosyl-(1→2)-δ-fructofuranoside, indicates four things:

- Its monosaccharides: glucose and fructose
- Their ring types: glucose is a pyranose, and fructose is a furanose
- How they are linked together: the oxygen on carbon number 1 (C1) of α-δ-glucose is linked to the C2 of δ-fructose.
- The *-oside* suffix indicates that the anomeric carbon of both monosaccharides participates in the glycosidic bond.

Lactose, a disaccharide composed of one δ-galactose molecule and one δ-glucose molecule, occurs naturally in mammalian milk. The systematic name for lactose is *O*-ß-δ-galactopyranosyl-(1→4)-δ-glucopyranose. Other notable disaccharides include maltose (two δ-glucoses linked α-1, 4) and cellulobiose (two δ-glucoses linked ß-1, 4).

9 Starch

Starch or amylum [CAS 9005-25-8, chemical formula $(C_6H_{10}O_5)_n$] is a polysaccharide carbohydrate consisting of a large number of glucose units joined together by glycosidic bonds. Starch is produced by all green plants as an energy store and is a major food source for humans.

Pure starch is a white, tasteless and odorless powder that is insoluble in cold water or alcohol. It consists of two types of molecules: the linear and helical amylose and the branched amylopectin. Depending on the plant, starch generally contains 20 to 25% amylose and 75 to 80% amylopectin Glycogen, the glucose store of animals, is a more branched version of amylopectin.

The word "starch" is derived from Middle English *sterchen*, meaning to stiffen, which is appropriate since starch can be used as a thickening or glueing agent when dissolved in water and heated, giving wheatpaste.

Energy Store of Plants

In photosynthesis, plants use light energy to produce glucose from carbon dioxide. The glucose is stored mainly in the form of starch granules, in plastids such as chloroplasts and especially amyloplasts. Toward the end of the growing season, starch accumulates in twigs of trees near the buds. Fruit, seeds, rhizomes, and tubers store starch to prepare for the next growing season.

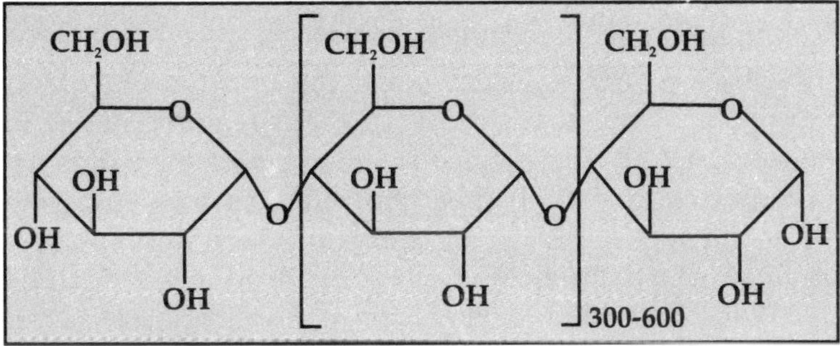

Fig. 9.1: **Structure of the amylose molecule**

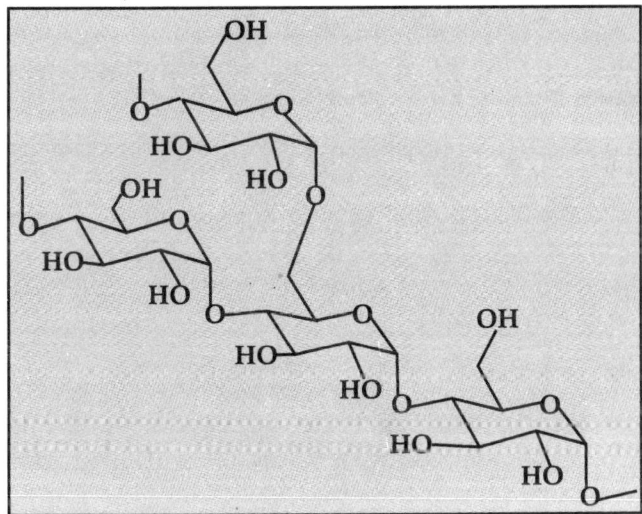

Fig. 9.2: **Structure of the amylopectin molecule**

Glucose is soluble in water, hydrophilic, binds much water and takes up much space; however, glucose in the form of starch, on the other hand, is not soluble and can be stored much more compactly.

Biosynthesis

Plants produce starch by first converting glucose 1-phosphate to ADP-glucose using the enzyme glucose-1-phosphate adenylyltransferase. This step requires energy in the form of ATP. The enzyme starch synthase then adds the ADP-glucose via a 1, 4-alpha glycosidic bond to a growing chain of glucose residues, liberating ADP and creating amylose. Starch branching enzyme introduces 1, 6-alpha glycosidic bonds between these chains, creating the branched amylopectin. The starch debranching enzyme isoamylase removes some of these branches. Several isoforms of these enzymes exist, leading to a highly complex synthesis process.

While amylose was traditionally thought to be completely unbranched, it is now known that some of its molecules contain a few branch points.

Glycogen and amylopectin have the same structure, but the former has about one branch point per ten 1, 4-alpha bonds, compared to about one branch point per thirty 1, 4-alpha bonds in amylopectin. Another difference is that glycogen is synthesised from UDP-glucose while starch is synthesised from ADP-glucose.

Starch as Food

Starch is the most important carbohydrate in the human diet. The major sources of starch intake worldwide are rice, wheat, maize (corn), potatoes and cassava. Widely used prepared foods containing starch are bread, pancakes, cereals, noodles, pasta and tortilla.

Depending on the local climate other starch sources are used for food, such as arrowroot, arracacha, buckwheat, barley, oat, millet, rey, banana, malanga, kudzu, oca, sago, sorghum, sweet potato, canna, taro and yams. Chestnuts and edible beans, such as favas, lentils, mung bean and peas, are also rich in starch.

The starch industry extracts and refines starches from seeds, roots and tubers, by wet grinding, sieving and drying. Today, the main commercial refined starches are cornstarch, tapioca, wheat and potato starch. To a lesser extent, sources include rice, sweet potato, sago and mung bean. Historically, Florida arrowroot was also commercialized. Still starch is extracted from more than 50 types of plants.

Alpha-amylases are the enzymes that break down starch into the constituent sugars. They are found in plants and in animals. Human saliva is rich in amylase, and the pancreas also excretes the enzyme. Individuals from populations with a high-starch diet tend to have more amylase genes than those with low-starch diets; chimpanzees have very few amylase genes. It is possible that turning to a high-starch diet was a significant event in human evolution.

Resistant starch is starch that escapes digestion in the small intestine of healthy individuals.

Modified Starch

A modified food starch undergoes one or more chemical modifications, which allow the starch for example to function properly such as under high heat and/or shear, frequently encountered during processing, and conditions during storage, such as cooling.

When a starch is pre-cooked, it can then be used to thicken instantly in cold water. This is referred to as a pregelatinized starch. Otherwise starch requires heat to thicken, or "gelatinize". The actual temperature depends on the type of starch.

The modified starches are coded according to the International Numbering System for Food Additives (INS):

- 1401 Acid-treated starch
- 1402 Alkaline-treated starch
- 1403 Bleached starch
- 1404 Oxidized starch
- 1405 Starches, enzyme-treated
- 1410 Monostarch phosphate
- 1411 Distarch glycerol
- 1412 Distarch phosphate esterified with sodium trimetaphosphate
- 1413 Phosphated distarch phosphate
- 1414 Acetylated distarch phosphate
- 1420 Starch acetate esterified with acetic anhydride
- 1421 Starch acetate esterified with vinyl acetate
- 1422 Acetylated distarch adipate
- 1423 Acetylated distarch glycerol
- 1440 Hydroxypropyl starch
- 1442 Hydroxypropyl distarch phosphate
- 1443 Hydroxypropyl distarch glycerol
- 1450 Starch sodium octenyl succinate

Some other types of modified starches commercially available are dextrins, cationic starches, carboxymethylated starches.

Use as Food Additive

As an additive for food processing, food starches are typically used as thickeners and stabilizers in foods such as puddings, custards, soups, sauces, gravies, pie fillings, and salad dressings, and to make noodles and pastas.

But by far the most common starch based food ingredient are starch sugars (see below) used as sweetener in many drinks and foods.

Use as a mold. Gummed sweets such as jelly beans and wine gums are not manufactured using a mold in the conventional sense. A tray is filled with native starch and leveled. A positive mold is then pressed into the starch leaving an impression of 1000 or so jelly beans. The mix is then poured into the impressions and then put into a stove to set. This method greatly reduces the number of molds that must be manufactured.

Starch is used as an excipient, a binder in medications to aid the formation of tablets.

Starch Sugars

Starch can be hydrolyzed into simpler carbohydrates by acids, various enzymes, or a combination of the two. The extent of conversion is typically quantified by Dextrose Equivalency (DE), which is roughly the fraction of the glycosidic bonds in starch that have been broken. Food products made in this way include:

- Maltodextrin, a lightly hydrolyzed (DE 10-20) starch product used as a bland-tasting filler and thickener.
- Various glucose syrup/corn syrups (DE 30-70), viscous solutions used as sweeteners and thickeners in many kinds of processed foods.
- Dextrose (DE 100), commercial glucose, prepared by the complete hydrolysis of starch.
- High fructose syrup, made by treating dextrose solutions with the enzyme glucose isomerase, until a substantial fraction of the glucose has been converted to fructose. In the United States, high fructose corn syrup is the principal sweetener used in sweetened beverages because fructose has better handling

characteristics, such as microbiological stability, and more consistent sweetness/flavor. High fructose corn syrup has the same sweetness as sugar.

- Sugar alcohols, such as maltitol, erythritol, sorbitol, mannitol, are sweeteners made by reducing sugars.

Industrial Applications

Papermaking is the largest non-food application for starches globally, consuming millions of metric tons annually. In a typical sheet of copy paper for instance, the starch content may be as high as 8%. Both chemically modified and unmodified starches are used in papermaking. In the wet part of the papermaking process, generally called the "wet-end", the starches used are cationic and have a positive charge bound to the starch polymer. These starch derivatives associate with the anionic or negatively charged paper fibers/ cellulose and inorganic fillers. Cationic starches together with other retention and internal sizing agent help to give the necessary strength properties to the paper web to be formed in the papermaking process (wet strength), and to provide strength to the final paper sheet (dry strength).

In the dry end of the papermaking process the paper web is rewetted with a starch based solution. The process is called surface sizing. Starches used have been chemically, or enzymatically depolymerized at the paper mill or by the starch industry (oxidized starch). The size - starch solutions are applied to the paper web by means of various mechanical presses (size press). Together with surface sizing agent the surface starches impart additional strength to the paper web and additionally provide water hold out or "size" for superior printing properties. Starch is also used in paper coating as one of the binders for the coating formulation a mixture of pigments, binders and thickeners. Coated paper has improved smoothness, hardness, whiteness and gloss and thus improves printing characteristics.

Corrugated Board Adhesives

Corrugated board adhesives are the next largest application of non-food starches globally. Starch glues are mostly based on unmodified native starches plus some additive as borax and caustic soda. Part of the starch is gelatinized to carrier slurry of uncooked starches and prevent sedimentation. This opaque glue is called a Stein Hall adhesives. The glue is applied on tips of the fluting. The fluted paper is pressed to paper called liner. This is then dried under high heat, which causes the rest of the uncooked starch in glue to swell/gelatinize. This gelatinizing makes the glue a fast and strong for corrugated board production.

Another large non-food starch application is in the construction industry where starch is used in the gypsum wall board manufacturing process. Chemically modified or unmodified starches are added to the stucco containing primarily gypsum. Top and bottom heavyweight sheets of paper are applied to the formulation and the process is allowed to heat and cure to form the eventual rigid wall board. The starches act as a glue for the cured gypsum rock with the paper covering and also provide rigidity to the board.

Adhesives

Starch is used in the manufacture of various glues for book-binding, wallpaper adhesives, paper sack production, tube winding, gummed paper, envelop adhesives, school glues, bottle labeling.

Starch derivatives as yellow dextrins can be modified by addition of some chemical forms to be a hard glue for paper work, some of those forms are Borax, Soda Ash, which mixed with the starch solution at 50-70 °C to gain a very good adhesive, Sodium Silicate can be added to reinforce this formula.

Clothing Starch or Laundry Starch

Clothing starch or laundry starch is a liquid that is prepared by mixing a vegetable starch in water (earlier preparations also had to be boiled), and is used in the laundering of clothes. Starch was widely used in Europe in the 16th and 17th centuries to stiffen the wide collars and ruffs of fine linen which surrounded the necks of the well-to-do. During the 19th century and early 20th century, it was stylish to stiffen the collars and sleeves of men's shirts and the ruffles of girls' petticoats by applying starch to them as the clean clothes were being ironed. Aside from the smooth, crisp edges it gave to clothing, it served practical purposes as well. Dirt and sweat from a person's neck and wrists would stick to the starch rather than to the fibers of the clothing, and would easily wash away along with the starch. After each laundering, the starch would be reapplied. Today the product is sold in aerosol cans for home use.

Starch is also used to make some packing peanuts, and some dropped ceiling tiles.

Textile Chemicals

To reduce breaking of yarns during weaving, the warp yarns are sized. Starch is one of the main agents used for cotton sizing. Starch is also used as printing thickener.

Printing Industry

Printing industry in the printing industry food grade starch is used in the manufacture of anti-set-off spray powder used to separate printed sheets of paper to avoid wet ink being set off.

Bioplastics

Bioplastics starch is used to produce various bioplastics, synthetic polymers that are biodegradable. An example is polylactic acid.

Body Powder

Powdered corn starch is used as a substitute for talcum powder in many health and beauty products.

Oil Exploration

Oil exploration starch is used to adjust the viscosity of drilling fluid which is used to lubricate the drill head in (mineral) oil extraction.

Bio-ethanol

Glucose from starch can be further fermented to ethanol.

Hydrogen Production

Starch can be used to produce hydrogen, using enzymes.

Tests

Iodine solution is used to test for starch; a blue color indicates the presence of starch. The details of this reaction are not yet fully known, but it is thought that the iodine (I3- and I5- ions) fits inside the coils of amylose, the charge transfers between the iodine and the starch, and the energy level spacings in the resulting complex correspond to the absorption spectrum in the visible light region. The strength of the resulting blue color depends on the amount of amylose present.

Starch indicator solution consisting of water, starch and iodine is often used in redox titrations: in the presence of an oxidizing agent the solution turns blue, in the presence of reducing agent the blue color disappears because triiodide (I3-) ions break up into three iodide ions, disassembling the starch-iodine complex. A 0.3% w/w solution is the standard concentration for a starch indicator. It is made by adding 4 grams of soluble starch to 1 litre of heated water; the solution is cooled before use (starch-iodine complex becomes unstable at temperatures above 35 °C).

Microscopy of Starch Granules

Each species of plant has a unique shape of starch granules in granular size, shape and crystallisation pattern. Under the microscope, starch grains stained with iodine illuminated from behind with polarized light show a distinctive Maltese cross effect (also known as extinction cross and birefringe.

Photosynthesis

Composite image showing the global distribution of photosynthesis, including both oceanic phytoplankton and terrestrial vegetation.

Photosynthesis is a metabolic pathway that converts carbon dioxide into organic compounds, especially sugars, using the energy from sunlight. Photosynthesis occurs in plants, algae, and many species of Bacteria, but not in Archaea. Photosynthetic organisms are called *photoautotrophs,* but not all organisms that use light as a source of energy carry out photosynthesis, since *photoheterotrophs* use organic compounds, rather than carbon dioxide, as a source of carbon In plants, algae and cyanobacteria photosynthesis uses carbon dioxide and water, releasing oxygen as a waste product. Photosynthesis is crucially important for life on Earth, since as well as it maintaining the normal level of oxygen in the atmosphere, nearly all life either depends on it directly as a source of energy, or indirectly as the ultimate source of the energy in their food The amount of energy trapped by photosynthesis is immense, approximately 100 terawatts which is about six times larger than the yearly power consumption of human civilization In all, photosynthetic organisms convert around 100,000,000,000 tonnes of carbon into biomass per year.

Although photosynthesis can occur in different ways in different species, some features are always the same. For example, the process always begins when energy from light is absorbed by proteins called photosynthetic reaction centers that contain chlorophyll. In plants these proteins are held inside organelles called chloroplasts, while in bacteria they are embedded in the plasma membrane. Some of the light energy gathered by chlorophylls is stored in the form of adenosine triphosphate (ATP). The rest of the energy is used to remove electrons from a substance such as water. These electrons are then used in the reactions that turn carbon dioxide into organic compounds. In plants, algae and cyanobacteria these reactions are called the Calvin cycle, but different sets of reactions can be found in bacteria, such as the reverse Krebs cycle in *Chlorobium*. Many photosynthetic organisms have adaptations that concentrate or store carbon dioxide, this helps reduce a wasteful process called photorespiration that would otherwise consume part of the sugar produced during photosynthesis.

Photosynthesis evolved early in the evolutionary history of life, when all forms of life on Earth were microorganisms. Although the dates are difficult to estimate with any accuracy, the first photosynthetic organisms probably evolved about 3,500 million years ago, and used hydrogen or hydrogen sulfide as sources of electrons, rather than water. Cyanobacteria appeared later, around 3,000 million years ago, and changed the Earth forever when they began to oxygenate the atmosphere, beginning about 2,400 million years ago This new atmosphere allowed the evolution of complex life such as protists. Eventually, about 550 million years ago, one of these protists formed a symbiotic relationship with a cyanobacterium, producing the ancestor of the plants and algae The chloroplasts in modern plants are the descendants of these ancient symbiotic cyanobacteria.

Overview

Photosynthetic organisms are photoautotrophs, which means that they are able to synthesize food directly from carbon dioxide using energy from light. In plants, algae and cyanobacteria, photosynthesis releases oxygen, this is called *oxygenic photosynthesis*. Although there are some differences between oxygenic photosynthesis in plants, algae and cyanobacteria, the overall process is quite similar in these organisms. However, there are some types of bacteria that carry out *anoxygenic photosynthesis*, which consumes carbon dioxide but does not release oxygen.

Carbon dioxide is converted into sugars in a process called carbon fixation. Carbon fixation is a redox reaction, so photosynthesis needs to supply both a source of energy to drive this process, and also the electrons needed to convert carbon dioxide into carbohydrate, which is a reduction reaction. In general outline, photosynthesis is the opposite of cellular respiration, where glucose and other compounds are oxidized to produce carbon dioxide, water, and release chemical energy. However, the two processes take place through a different sequence of chemical reactions and in different cellular compartments.

The general equation for photosynthesis is therefore:

$$CO_2 + 2\ H_2A + \text{photons} \rightarrow (CH_2O)_n + H_2O + 2A \quad (9.1)$$

carbon dioxide + electron donor + light energy → carbohydrate + oxygen + oxidized electron donor

Since water is most often used as the electron donor in oxygenic photosynthesis, the equation for this process is:

$$CO_2 + 2\ H_2O + \text{photons} \rightarrow (CH_2O)_n + H_2O + O_2 \quad (9.2)$$

carbon dioxide + water + light energy → carbohydrate + oxygen + water

Other processes (e.g. as used by microbial species in Mono Lake, California) substitute other compounds (such as arsenite) for water in the electron-supply role; the microbes use sunlight to reduce arsenite to arsenate The equation for this reaction is:

$$(AsO_3^{3-}) + CO_2 + \text{photons} \rightarrow CO + (AsO_4^{3-}) \quad (9.3)$$

carbon dioxide + arsenite + light energy → arsenate + carbon monoxide (used to build other compounds in subsequent reactions)

Photosynthesis occurs in two stages. In the first stage, *light-dependent reactions* or *light reactions* capture the energy of light and use it to make the energy-storage molecules ATP and NADPH. During the second stage, the *light-independent reactions* use these products to capture and reduce carbon dioxide.

Photosynthetic Membranes and Organelles

The proteins that gather light for photosynthesis are embedded within cell membranes. The simplest way these are arranged is in photosynthetic bacteria, where these proteins are held within the plasma membrane However, this membrane may be tightly-folded into cylindrical sheets called thylakoids, or bunched up into round vesicles called *intracytoplasmic membranes* These structures can fill most of the interior of a cell, giving the membrane a very large surface area and therefore increasing the amount of light that the bacteria can absorb.

In plants and algae, photosynthesis takes place in organelles called chloroplasts. A chloroplast is contained by an envelope that consists of an inner and an outer phospholipid membrane. Between these two layers is the intermembrane space. A typical plant cell contains about 10 to 100 chloroplasts. Within the stroma are stacks of thylakoids, the sub-organelles which are the site of photosynthesis. The thylakoids are arranged in stacks called grana (singular: granum). A thylakoid has a flattened disk shape. Inside it is an empty area called the thylakoid space or lumen. The thylakoid membrane contains many integral and peripheral membrane proteins. The proteins complexes which contain special pigments absorbing light energy are called photosystems.

Plants absorb light primarily using the pigment chlorophyll, which is the reason that most plants have a green colour. Besides chlorophyll, plants also use pigments such as carotenes and xanthophylls. Algae also use chlorophyll, but various other pigments are present as phycocyanin, carotenes, and xanthophylls in green algae, phycoerythrin in red algae (rhodophytes) and fucoxanthol in brown algae and diatoms resulting in a wide variety of colors.

These pigments are embedded in plants and algae in special antenna-proteins. In such proteins all the pigments are ordered to work well together. Such a protein is also called a light-harvesting complex.

Although all cells in the green parts of a plant have chloroplasts, most of the energy is captured in the leaves. The cells in the interior tissues of a leaf, called the mesophyll, can contain between 450,000 and 800,000 chloroplasts for every square millimeter of leaf. The surface of the leaf is uniformly coated with a water-resistant waxy cuticle that protects the leaf from excessive evaporation of water and decreases the absorption of ultraviolet or blue light to reduce heating. The transparent epidermis layer allows light to pass through to the palisade mesophyll cells where most of the photosynthesis takes place.

Light Reactions

In the light reactions, one molecule of the pigment chlorophyll absorbs one photon and loses one electron. This electron is passed to a modified form of chlorophyll called pheophytin, which passes the electron to a quinone molecule, allowing the start of a flow of electrons down an electron transport chain that leads to the ultimate reduction of NADP to NADPH. In addition, this creates a proton gradient across the chloroplast membrane; its dissipation is used by ATP synthase for the concomitant synthesis of ATP. The chlorophyll molecule regains the lost electron from a water molecule through a process called photolysis, which releases a dioxygen (O_2) molecule. The overall equation for the light-dependent reactions under the conditions of non-cyclic electron flow in green plants is:

$$2\ H_2O + 2\ NADP^+ + 2\ ADP + 2\ P_i + \text{light} \rightarrow 2\ NADPH + 2\ H^+ + 2\ ATP + O_2 \qquad (9.4)$$

Not all wavelengths of light can support photosynthesis. The photosynthetic action spectrum depends on the type of accessory pigments present. For example, in green plants, the action spectrum resembles the absorption spectrum for chlorophylls and carotenoids with peaks for violet-blue and red light. In red algae, the action spectrum overlaps with the absorption spectrum of phycobilins for blue-green light, which allows these algae to grow in deeper waters that filter out the longer wavelengths used by green plants. The non-absorbed part of the light spectrum is what gives photosynthetic organisms their color (e.g., green plants, red algae, purple bacteria) and is the least effective for photosynthesis in the respective organisms.

Z Scheme

In plants, light-dependent reactions occur in the thylakoid membranes of the chloroplasts and use light energy to synthesize ATP and NADPH. The light-dependent reaction has two forms; cyclic and non-cyclic reaction. In the non-cyclic reaction, the photons are captured in the light harvesting antenna complexes of photosystem II by chlorophyll and other accessory pigments. When a chlorophyll molecule at the core of the photosystem II reaction center obtains sufficient excitation energy from the adjacent antenna pigments, an electron is transferred to the primary electron-acceptor molecule, Pheophytin, through a process called Photoinduced charge separation. These electrons are shuttled through an electron transport chain, the so called *Z-scheme* shown in the diagram, that initially functions to generate a chemiosmotic potential across the membrane. An ATP synthase enzyme uses the chemiosmotic potential to make ATP during photophosphorylation, whereas NADPH is a product of the terminal redox reaction in the *Z-scheme*. The electron enters the Photosystem I molecule. The electron is excited due to the light absorbed by the photosystem. A second electron carrier accepts the electron, which again is passed down lowering energies of electron acceptors. The energy created by the electron acceptors is used to move hydrogen ions across the thylakoid membrane into the lumen. The electron is used to reduce the co-enzyme NADP, which has functions in the light-independent reaction. The cyclic reaction is similar to that of the non-cyclic, but differs in the form that it generates only ATP, and no reduced NADP (NADPH) is created. The cyclic reaction takes place only at photosystem I. Once the electron is displaced from the photosystem, the electron is passed down the electron acceptor molecules and returns back to photosystem I, from where it was emitted, hence the name *cyclic reaction*.

Water Photolysis

The NADPH is the main reducing agent in chloroplasts, providing a source of energetic electrons to other reactions. Its production leaves chlorophyll with a deficit of electrons (oxidized), which must be obtained from some other reducing agent. The excited electrons lost from chlorophyll in photosystem I are replaced from the electron transport chain by plastocyanin. However, since photosystem II includes the first steps of the *Z-scheme*, an external source of electrons is required to reduce its oxidized chlorophyll a molecules. The source of electrons in green-plant and cyanobacterial photosynthesis is water. Two water molecules are oxidized by four successive charge-separation reactions by photosystem II to yield a molecule of diatomic oxygen and four hydrogen ions; the electron yielded in each step is transferred to a redox-active tyrosine residue that then reduces the photoxidized paired-chlorophyll *a* species called P680 that serves as the primary (light-driven) electron donor in the photosystem II reaction center. The oxidation of water is catalyzed in photosystem II by a redox-active structure that contains four manganese ions and a calcium ion; this oxygen-evolving complex binds two water molecules and stores the four oxidizing equivalents that are required to drive the water-oxidizing reaction. Photosystem II is the only known biological enzyme that carries out this oxidation of water. The hydrogen ions contribute to the transmembrane chemiosmotic potential that leads to ATP synthesis. Oxygen is a waste product of light-dependent reactions, but the majority of organisms on Earth use oxygen for cellular respiration, including photosynthetic organisms

Oxygen and Photosynthesis

With respect to oxygen and photosynthesis, there are two important concepts.

1. Plant and cyanobacterial (blue-green algae) cells also use oxygen for cellular respiration, although they have a net output of oxygen since much more is produced during photosynthesis.
2. Oxygen is a product of the light-driven water-oxidation reaction catalyzed by photosystem II; it is not generated by the fixation of carbon dioxide. Consequently, the source of oxygen during photosynthesis is water, not carbon dioxide.

The concept that oxygen production is not directly associated with the fixation of carbon dioxide was first proposed by Cornelis Van Niel in the 1930s, who studied photosynthetic bacteria. Aside from the cyanobacteria, bacteria only have one photosystem and use reducing agents other than water. They get electrons from a variety of different inorganic chemicals including sulfide or hydrogen, so for most of these bacteria oxygen is not produced.

Others, such as the halophiles (an Archaea), produced so-called purple membranes where the bacteriorhodopsin could harvest light and produce energy. The purple membranes was one of the first to be used to demonstrate the chemiosmotic theory: light hit the membranes and the pH of the solution that contained the purple membranes dropped as protons were pumping out of the membrane.

LIGHT-INDEPENDENT REACTIONS

The Calvin Cycle

In the Light-independent or dark reactions the enzyme RuBisCO captures CO_2 from the atmosphere and in a process that requires the newly formed NADPH, called the Calvin-Benson Cycle, releases three-carbon sugars, which are later combined to form sucrose and starch. The overall equation for the light-independent reactions in green plants is:

$$3\,CO_2 + 9\,ATP + 6\,NADPH + 6\,H^+ \rightarrow C_3H_6O_3\text{-phosphate} + 9\,ADP + 8\,P_i + 6\,NADP^+ + 3\,H_2O \qquad (9.5)$$

To be more specific, carbon fixation produces an intermediate product, which is then converted to the final carbohydrate products. The carbon skeletons produced by photosynthesis are then variously used to form other organic compounds, such as the building material cellulose, as precursors for lipid and amino acid biosynthesis, or as a fuel in cellular respiration. The latter occurs not only in plants but also in animals when the energy from plants gets passed through a food chain.

The fixation or reduction of carbon dioxide is a process in which carbon dioxide combines with a five-carbon sugar, ribulose 1, 5-bisphosphate (RuBP), to yield two molecules of a three-carbon compound, glycerate 3-phosphate (GP), also known as 3-phosphoglycerate (PGA). GP, in the presence of

ATP and NADPH from the light-dependent stages, is reduced to glyceraldehyde 3-phosphate (G3P). This product is also referred to as 3-phosphoglyceraldehyde (PGAL) or even as triose phosphate. Triose is a 3-carbon sugar (see carbohydrates). Most (5 out of 6 molecules) of the G3P produced is used to regenerate RuBP so the process can continue (see Calvin-Benson cycle). The 1 out of 6 molecules of the triose phosphates not "recycled" often condense to form hexose phosphates, which ultimately yield sucrose, starch and cellulose. The sugars produced during carbon metabolism yield carbon skeletons that can be used for other metabolic reactions like the production of amino acids and lipids.

C_4 and C_3 Photosynthesis and CAM

In hot and dry conditions, plants will close their stomata to prevent loss of water. Under these conditions, CO_2 will decrease, and dioxygen gas, produced by the light reactions of photosynthesis, will increase in the leaves, causing an increase of photorespiration by the oxygenase activity of ribulose-1, 5-bisphosphate carboxylase/oxygenase and decrease in carbon fixation. Some plants have evolved mechanisms to increase the CO_2 concentration in the leaves under these conditions.

C_4 plants chemically fix carbon dioxide in the cells of the mesophyll by adding it to the three-carbon molecule phosphoenolpyruvate (PEP), a reaction catalyzed by an enzyme called PEP carboxylase and which creates the four-carbon organic acid, oxaloacetic acid. Oxaloacetic acid or malate synthesized by this process is then translocated to specialized bundle sheath cells where the enzyme, rubisco, and other Calvin cyle enzymes are located, and where CO_2 released by decarboxylation of the four-carbon acids is then fixed by rubisco activity to the three-carbon sugar 3-Phosphoglyceric acids. The physical separation of rubisco from the oxygen-generating light reactions reduces photorespiration and increases CO_2 fixation and thus photosynthetic capacity of the leaf. C_4 plants can produce more sugar than C_3 plants in conditions of high light and temperature. Many important crop plants are C4 plants including maize, sorghum, sugarcane, and millet. Plants lacking PEP-carboxylase are called *C_3 plants* because the primary carboxylation reaction, catalyzed by Rubiso, produces the three-carbon sugar 3-phosphoglyceric acids directly in the Calvin-Benson Cycle.

Xerophytes such as cacti and most succulents also use PEP carboxylase to capture carbon dioxide in a process called Crassulacean acid metabolism (CAM). In contrast to C_4 metabolism, which *physically* separates the CO_2 fixation to PEP from the Calvin cycle, CAM only *temporally* separates these two processes. CAM plants have a different leaf anatomy than C4 plants, and fix the CO_2 at night, when their stomata are open. CAM plants store the CO_2 mostly in the form of malic acid via carboxylation of phosphoenolpyruvate to oxaloacetate, which is then reduced to malate. Decarboxylation of malate during the day releases CO_2 inside the leaves thus allowing carbon fixation to 3-phosphoglycerate by rubisco.

Order and Kinetics

The overall process of photosynthesis takes place in four stages. The first, energy transfer in antenna chlorophyll takes place in the femtosecond [1 femtosecond (fs) = 10,-15 s] to picosecond [1 picosecond (ps) = 10-12 s] time scale. The next phase, the transfer of electrons in photochemical reactions, takes place in the picosecond to nanosecond time scale [1 nanosecond (ns) = 10-9 s]. The third phase, the electron transport chain and ATP synthesis, takes place on the microsecond [1 microsecond (µs) = 10-6 s] to millisecond [1 millisecond (ms) = 10-3 s) time scale. The final phase is carbon fixation and export of stable products and takes place in the millisecond to second time scale. The first three stages occur in the thylakoid membranes.

Efficiency

Plants usually convert light into chemical energy with a photosynthetic efficiency of 3-6% Actual plant's photosynthetic efficiency varies with the frequency of the light being converted, light intensity, temperature and proportion of CO_2 in atmosphere, and can vary from 0.1% to 8% By comparison, solar panels convert light into electric energy at a photosynthetic efficiency of approximately 6-20% for mass produced panels, and up to 41% in a research laboratory.

Evolution

Early photosynthetic systems, such as those from green and purple sulfur and green and purple non-sulfur bacteria, are thought to have been anoxygenic, using various molecules as electron donors. Green and purple sulfur bacteria are thought to have used hydrogen and sulfur as an electron donor. Green nonsulfur bacteria used various amino and other organic acids. Purple nonsulfur bacteria used a variety of non-specific organic molecules. The use of these molecules is consistent with the geological evidence that the atmosphere was highly reduced at that time.

Fossils of what are thought to be filamentous photosynthetic organisms have been dated at 3.4 billion years old.

The main source of oxygen in the atmosphere is oxygenic photosynthesis, and its first appearance is sometimes referred to as the oxygen catastrophe. Geological evidence suggests that oxygenic photosynthesis, such as that in cyanobacteria, became important during the Paleoproterozoic era around 2 billion years ago. Modern photosynthesis in plants and most photosynthetic prokaryotes is oxygenic. Oxygenic photosynthesis uses water as an electron donor which is oxidized to molecular dioxygen (O_2) in the photosynthetic reaction center.

Symbiosis and the Origin of Chloroplasts

Several groups of animals have formed symbiotic relationships with photosynthetic algae. These are most common in corals, sponges and sea anemones, possibly due to these animals having particularly simple body plans and large surface areas compared to their volumes. In addition, a few marine molluscs *Elysia viridis* and *Elysia chlorotica* also maintain a symbiotic relationship with chloroplasts that they capture from the algae in their diet and then store in their bodies. This allows the molluscs to survive solely by photosynthesis for several months at a time. Some of the genes from the plant cell nucleus have even been transferred to the slugs, so that the chloroplasts can be supplied with proteins that they need to survive.

An even closer form of symbiosis may explain the origin of chloroplasts. Chloroplasts have many similarities with photosynthetic bacteria including a circular chromosome, prokaryotic-type ribosomes, and similar proteins in the photosynthetic reaction centre. The endosymbiotic theory suggests that photosynthetic bacteria were acquired (by endocytosis) by early eukaryotic cells to form the first plant cells. Therefore, chloroplasts may be photosynthetic bacteria that adapted to life inside plant cells. Like mitochondria, chloroplasts still possess their own DNA, separate from the nuclear DNA of their plant host cells and the genes in this chloroplast DNA resemble those in cyanobacteria DNA in chloroplasts codes for redox proteins such as photosynthetic reaction centers. The CoRR Hypothesis proposes that this Co-location is required for Redox Regulation.

Cyanobacteria and the Evolution of Photosynthesis

The biochemical capacity to use water as the source for electrons in photosynthesis evolved once, in a common ancestor of extant cyanobacteria. The geological record indicates that this transforming event took place early in Earth's history, at least 2450-2320 million years ago (Ma), and possibly much earlier. Available evidence from geobiological studies of Archean (>2500 Ma) sedimentary rocks indicates that life existed 3500 Ma, but the question of when oxygenic photosynthesis evolved is still unanswered. A clear paleontological window on cyanobacterial evolution opened about 2000 Ma, revealing an already-diverse biota of blue-greens. Cyanobacteria remained principal primary producers throughout the Proterozoic Eon (2500-543 Ma), in part because the redox structure of the oceans favoured photoautotrophs capable of nitrogen fixation. Green algae joined blue-greens as major primary producers on continental shelves near the end of the Proterozoic, but only with the Mesozoic (251-65 Ma) radiations of dinoflagellates, coccolithophorids, and diatoms did primary production in marine shelf waters take modern form. Cyanobacteria remain critical to marine ecosystems as primary producers in oceanic gyres, as agents of biological nitrogen fixation, and, in modified form, as the plastids of marine algae.

Discovery

Although some of the steps in photosynthesis are still not completely understood, the overall photosynthetic equation has been known since the 1800s.

Jan van Helmont began the research of the process in the mid-1600s when he carefully measured the mass of the soil used by a plant and the mass of the plant as it grew. After noticing that the soil mass changed very little, he hypothesized that the mass of the growing plant must come from the water, the only substance he added to the potted plant. His hypothesis was partially accurate—much of the gained mass also comes from carbon dioxide as well as water. However, this was a signaling point to the idea that the bulk of a plant's biomass comes from the inputs of photosynthesis, not the soil itself.

Joseph Priestley, a chemist and minister, discovered that when he isolated a volume of air under an inverted jar, and burned a candle in it, the candle would burn out very quickly, much before it ran out of wax. He further discovered that a mouse could similarly "injure" air. He then showed that the air that had been "injured" by the candle and the mouse could be restored by a plant.

In 1778, Jan Ingenhousz, court physician to the Austrian Empress, repeated Priestley's experiments. He discovered that it was the influence of sunlight on the plant that could cause it to rescue a mouse in a matter of hours.

In 1796, Jean Senebier, a Swiss pastor, botanist, and naturalist, demonstrated that green plants consume carbon dioxide and release oxygen under the influence of light. Soon afterwards, Nicolas-Théodore de Saussure showed that the increase in mass of the plant as it grows could not be due only to uptake of CO_2, but also to the incorporation of water. Thus the basic reaction by which photosynthesis is used to produce food (such as glucose) was outlined.

Cornelis Van Niel made key discoveries explaining the chemistry of photosynthesis. By studying purple sulfur bacteria and green bacteria he was the first scientist to demonstrate that photosynthesis is a light-dependent redox reaction, in which hydrogen reduces carbon dioxide.

Robert Emerson discovered two light reactions by testing plant productivity using different wavelengths of light. With the red alone, the light reactions were suppressed. When blue and red were combined, the output was much more substantial. Thus, there were two photosystems, one aborbing up to 600 nm wavelengths, the other up to 700. The former is known as PSII, the latter is PSI. PSI contains only chlorophyll a, PSII contains primarily chlorophyll a with most of the available chlorophyll b, among other pigments.

Further experiments to prove that the oxygen developed during the photosynthesis of green plants came from water, were performed by Robert Hill in 1937 and 1939. He showed that isolated chloroplasts give off oxygen in the presence of unnatural reducing agents like iron oxalate, ferricyanide or benzoquinone after exposure to light. The Hill reaction is as follows:

$$2\ H_2O + 2\ A + \text{(light, chloroplasts)} \rightarrow 2\ AH_2 + O_2$$

where A is the electron acceptor. Therefore, in light the electron acceptor is reduced and oxygen is evolved. Cyt b_6, now known as a plastoquinone, is one electron acceptor.

Samuel Ruben and Martin Kamen used radioactive isotopes to determine that the oxygen liberated in photosynthesis came from the water.

Melvin Calvin and Andrew Benson, along with James Bassham, elucidated the path of carbon assimilation (the photosynthetic carbon reduction cycle) in plants. The carbon reduction cycle is known as the Calvin cycle, which inappropriately ignores the contribution of Bassham and Benson. Many scientists refer to the cycle as the Calvin-Benson Cycle, Benson-Calvin, and some even call it the Calvin-Benson-Bassham (or CBB) Cycle.

A Nobel Prize winning scientist, Rudolph A. Marcus, was able to discover the function and significance of the electron transport chain.

Factors

There are three main factors affecting photosynthesis and several corollary factors. The three main are:

- Light irradiance and wavelength
- Carbon dioxide concentration
- Temperature.

Light Intensity (irradiance), Wavelength and Temperature

In the early 1900s Frederick Frost Blackman along with Gabrielle Matthaei investigated the effects of light intensity (irradiance) and temperature on the rate of carbon assimilation.

- At constant temperature, the rate of carbon assimilation varies with irradiance, initially increasing as the irradiance increases. However at higher irradiance this relationship no longer holds and the rate of carbon assimilation reaches a plateau.
- At constant irradiance, the rate of carbon assimilation increases as the temperature is increased over a limited range. This effect is only seen at high irradiance levels. At low irradiance, increasing the temperature has little influence on the rate of carbon assimilation.

These two experiments illustrate vital points: firstly, from research it is known that photochemical reactions are not generally affected by temperature. However, these experiments clearly show that temperature affects the rate of carbon assimilation, so there must be two sets of reactions in the full process of carbon assimilation. These are of course the light-dependent 'photochemical' stage and the light-independent, temperature-dependent stage. Second, Blackman's experiments illustrate the concept of limiting factors. Another limiting factor is the wavelength of light. Cyanobacteria, which reside several meters underwater, cannot receive the correct wavelengths required to cause photoinduced charge separation in conventional photosynthetic pigments. To combat this problem, a series of proteins with different pigments surround the reaction center. This unit is called a phycobilisome.

Carbon Dioxide Levels and Photorespiration

As carbon dioxide concentrations rise, the rate at which sugars are made by the light-independent reactions increases until limited by other factors. RuBisCO, the enzyme that captures carbon dioxide in the light-independent reactions, has a binding affinity for both carbon dioxide and oxygen. When the concentration of carbon dioxide is high, RuBisCO will fix carbon dioxide. However, if the carbon dioxide concentration is low, RuBisCO will bind oxygen instead of carbon dioxide. This process, called photorespiration, uses energy, but does not produce sugars.

RuBisCO oxygenase activity is disadvantageous to plants for several reasons:

- One product of oxygenase activity is phosphoglycolate (2 carbon) instead of 3-phosphoglycerate (3 carbon). Phosphoglycolate cannot be metabolized by the Calvin-Benson cycle and represents carbon lost from the cycle. A high oxygenase activity, therefore, drains the sugars that are required to recycle ribulose 5-bisphosphate and for the continuation of the Calvin-Benson cycle.
- Phosphoglycolate is quickly metabolized to glycolate that is toxic to a plant at a high concentration; it inhibits photosynthesis.
- Salvaging glycolate is an energetically expensive process that uses the glycolate pathway and only 75% of the carbon is returned to the Calvin-Benson cycle as 3-phosphoglycerate. The reactions also produce ammonia (NH_3) which is able to diffuse out of the plant leading to a loss of nitrogen.

A highly-simplified summary is:

2 glycolate + ATP $\rightarrow$ 3-phosphoglycerate + carbon dioxide + ADP +NH_3

The salvaging pathway for the products of RuBisCO oxygenase activity is more commonly known as photorespiration, since it is characterized by light-dependent oxygen consumption and the release of carbon dioxide.

10 Cellulose

Cellulose is an organic compound with the formula $(C_6H_{10}O_5)_n$, a polysaccharide consisting of a linear chain of several hundred to over ten thousand ß linked δ-glucose units

Cellulose is the structural component of the primary cell wall of green plants, many forms of algae and the oomycetes. Some species of bacteria secrete it to form biofilms. Cellulose is the most common organic compound on Earth. About 33 per cent of all plant matter is cellulose (the cellulose content of cotton is 90 per cent and that of wood is 50 per cent).

For industrial use, cellulose is mainly obtained from wood pulp and cotton. It is mainly used to produce cardboard and paper; to a smaller extent it is converted into a wide variety of derivative products such as cellophane and rayon. Converting cellulose from energy crops into biofuels such as cellulosic ethanol is under investigation as an alternative fuel source.

Some animals, particularly ruminants and termites, can digest cellulose with the help of symbiotic micro-organisms that live in their guts. Cellulose is not digestible by humans and is often referred to as 'dietary fiber' or 'roughage', acting as a hydrophilic bulking agent for feces.

History

Cellulose was discovered in 1838 by the French chemist Anselme Payen, who isolated it from plant matter and determined its chemical formula Cellulose was used to produce the first successful thermoplastic polymer, celluloid, by Hyatt Manufacturing Company in 1870. Hermann Staudinger determined the polymer structure of cellulose in 1920. The compound was first chemically synthesized (without the use of any biologically-derived enzymes) in 1992, by Kobayashi and Shoda.

Commercial Products

Cellulose is the major constituent of paper and cardboard and of textiles made from cotton, linen, and other plant fibres.

Cellulose is the raw material in the manufacture of nitrocellulose (cellulose nitrate) which was historically used in smokeless gunpowder and as the base material for celluloid used for photographic and movie films until the mid 1930s.

Cellulose can be converted into cellophane, a thin transparent film, and into rayon, an important fiber that has been used for textiles since the beginning of the 20th century. Both cellophane and rayon are known as "regenerated cellulose fibres"; they are identical to cellulose in chemical structure and are usually made from viscose, a viscous solution made from cellulose. A more recent and environmentally friendly method to produce rayon is the Lyocell process.

Cellulose is used to make water-soluble adhesives and binders such as methyl cellulose and carboxymethyl cellulose which are used in wallpaper paste. Microcrystalline cellulose

(E460i) and powdered cellulose (E460ii) are used as inactive fillers in tablets and as thickeners and stabilizers in processed foods.

Cellulose insulation made from recycled newsprint is becoming popular as an environmentally preferable material for building insulation.

Cellulose is used in the laboratory as the stationary phase for thin layer chromatography. Cellulose fibres are also used in liquid filtration, sometimes in combination with diatomaceous earth or other filtration media, to create a filter bed of inert material. Cellulose is further used to make hydrophilic and highly absorbent sponges.

Cellulose Source and Energy Crops

The major combustible component of non-food energy crops is cellulose, with lignin second. Non-food energy crops are more efficient than edible energy crops (which have a large starch component), but still compete with food crops for agricultural land and water resources Typical non-food energy crops include industrial hemp, switchgrass, *Miscanthus*, *Salix* (willow), and *Populus* (poplar) species.

Some bacteria can convert cellulose into ethanol which can then be used as a fuel; see cellulosic ethanol.

Structure and Properties

Cellulose has no taste, is odourless, is hydrophilic, is insoluble in water and most organic solvents, is chiral and is biodegradable. It can be broken down chemically into its glucose units by treating it with concentrated acids at high temperature

Cellulose is derived from D-glucose units, which condense through ß(1→4)-glycosidic bonds. This linkage motif contrasts with that for a(1→4)-glycosidic bonds present in starch, glycogen, and other carbohydrates. Cellulose is a straight chain polymer: unlike starch, no coiling or branching occurs, and the molecule adopts an extended and rather stiff rod-like conformation, aided by the equatorial conformation of the glucose residues. The multiple hydroxyl groups on the glucose residues from one chain form hydrogen bonds with oxygen molecules on the same or on a neighbor chain, holding the chains firmly together side-by-side and forming *microfibrils* with high tensile strength. This strength is important in cell walls, where the microfibrils are meshed into a carbohydrate *matrix*, conferring rigidity to plant cells.

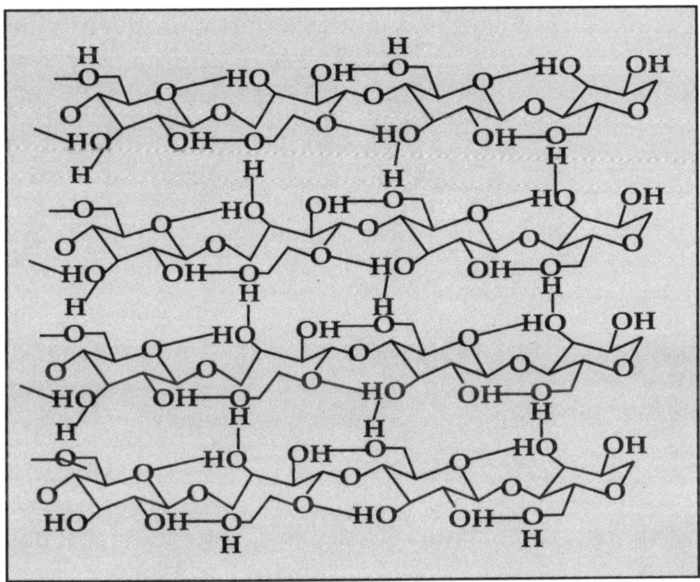

Fig. 10.1: **A strand of cellulose (conformation I_a), showing the hydrogen bonds (dashed) within and between cellulose molecules**

Compared to starch, cellulose is also much more crystalline. Whereas starch undergoes a crystalline to amorphous transition when heated beyond 60-70 °C in water (as in cooking), cellulose requires a temperature of 320 °C and pressure of 25 MPa to become amorphous in water.

Several different crystalline structures of cellulose are known, corresponding to the location of hydrogen bonds between and within strands. Natural cellulose is cellulose I, with structures I_α and I_β. Cellulose produced by bacteria and algae is enriched in I_a while cellulose of higher plants consists mainly of I_β. Cellulose in regenerated cellulose fibers is cellulose II. The conversion of cellulose I to cellulose II is not reversible, suggesting that cellulose I is metastable and cellulose II is stable. With various chemical treatments it is possible to produce the structures cellulose III and cellulose IV.

Many properties of cellulose depend on its chain length or degree of polymerization, the number of glucose units that make up one polymer molecule. Cellulose from wood pulp has typical chain lengths between 300 and 1700 units; cotton and other plant fibres as well as bacterial celluloses have chain lengths ranging from 800 to 10,000 units Molecules with very small chain length resulting from the breakdown of cellulose are known as cellodextrins; in contrast to long-chain cellulose, cellodextrins are typically soluble in water and organic solvents.

Plant-derived cellulose is usually contaminated with hemicellulose, lignin, pectin and other substances, while microbial cellulose is quite pure, has a much higher water content, and consists of long chains.

Cellulose is soluble in cupriethylenediamine (CED), cadmiumethylenediamine (Cadoxen), *N*-methylmorpholene *N*-oxide and lithium chloride/dimethylformamide . This is used in production of regenerated celluloses (as viscose and cellophane) from dissolving pulp.

Assaying Cellulose

Given a cellulose-containing material, the carbohydrate portion that does not dissolve in a 17.5% solution of sodium hydroxide at 20 °C is *a cellulose*, which is true cellulose. Acidification of the extract precipitates *ß cellulose*. The portion that dissolves in base but does not precipitate with acid is γ *cellulose*.

Cellulose can be assayed using a method described by Updegraff in 1969, where the fiber is dissolved in acetic and nitric acid to remove lignin, hemicellulose, and xylosans. The resulting cellulose is allowed to react with anthrone in sulfuric acid. The resulting coloured compound is assayed spectrophotometrically at a wavelength of approximately 635 nm.

In addition, cellulose is represented by the difference between acid detergent fiber (ADF) and acid detergent lignin (ADL).

Biosynthesis

In vascular plants cellulose is synthesized at the plasma membrane by rosette terminal complexes (RTC's). The RTC's are hexameric protein structures, approximately 25 nm in diameter, that contain the cellulose synthase enzymes that synthesise the individual cellulose chains Each RTC floats in the cell's plasma membrane and "spins" a microfibril into the cell wall.

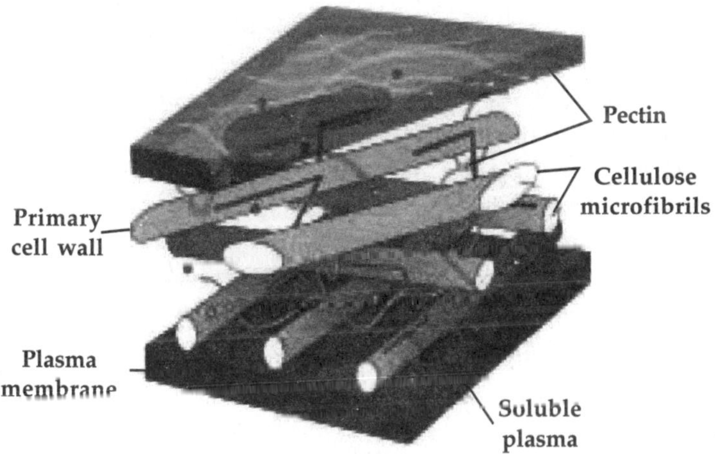

Fig. 10.2: **Location and arrangement of cellulose microfibrils in the plant cell wall.**

The RTC's contain at least three different cellulose synthases, encoded by *CesA* genes, in an unknown stoichiometry. Separate sets of *CesA* genes are involved in primary and secondary cell wall biosynthesis.

Cellulose synthesis requires chain initiation and elongation, and the two processes are separate. *CesA* glucosyltransferase initiates cellulose polymerization using a steroid primer, sitosterol-beta-glucoside, and UDP-glucose. Cellulose synthase utilizes UDP-δ-glucose precursors to elongate the growing cellulose chain. A cellulase may function to cleave the primer from the mature chain.

Breakdown (Cellulolysis)

Cellulolysis is the process of breaking down cellulose into smaller polysaccharides called cellodextrins or completely into glucose units; this is a hydrolysis reaction. Because cellulose molecules bind strongly to each other, cellulolysis is relatively difficult compared to the break down of other polysaccharides.

Mammals do not have the ability to break down cellulose directly. Some ruminants like cows and sheep contain certain symbiotic anaerobic bacteria (like *Cellulomonas*) in the flora of the gut wall, and these bacteria produce enzymes to break down cellulose; the break down products are then used by the mammal. Similarly, lower termites contain in their hindguts certain flagellate protozoa which produce such enzymes; higher termites contain bacteria for the job. Fungi, which in nature are responsible for recycling of nutrients, are also able to break down cellulose.

The enzymes utilized to cleave the glycosidic linkage in cellulose are glycoside hydrolases including endo-acting cellulases and exo-acting glucosidases. Such enzymes are usually secreted as part of multienzyme complexes that may include dockerins and cellulose binding modules; these complexes are in some cases referred to as cellulosomes.

Hemicellulose

Hemicellulose is a polysaccharide related to cellulose that comprises ca. 20% of the biomass of most plants. In contrast to cellulose, hemicellulose is derived from several sugars in addition to glucose, including especially xylose but also mannose, galactose, rhamnose, and arabinose. Hemicellulose consists of shorter chains - around 200 sugar units. Furthermore, hemicellulose is branched, whereas cellulose is unbranched.

Derivatives

The hydroxyl groups of cellulose can be partially or fully reacted with various reagents to afford derivatives with useful properties. Cellulose esters and cellulose ethers are the most important commercial materials. In principle, though not always in current industrial practice, cellulosic polymers are renewable resources.

Among the esters are cellulose acetate and cellulose triacetate, which are film- and fiber-forming materials that find a variety of uses. The inorganic ester nitrocellulose was initially used as an explosive and was an early film forming material.

Ether derivatives include:

- Ethylcellulose, a water-insoluble commercial thermoplastic used in coatings, inks, binders, and controlled-release drug tablets;
- Methylcellulose;
- Hydroxypropyl cellulose;
- Carboxymethyl cellulose;
- Hydroxypropyl methyl cellulose, E464, used as a viscosity modifier, gelling agent, foaming agent and binding agent; and
- Hydroxyethyl methyl cellulose, used in production of cellulose films.

Carbohydrate Reaction

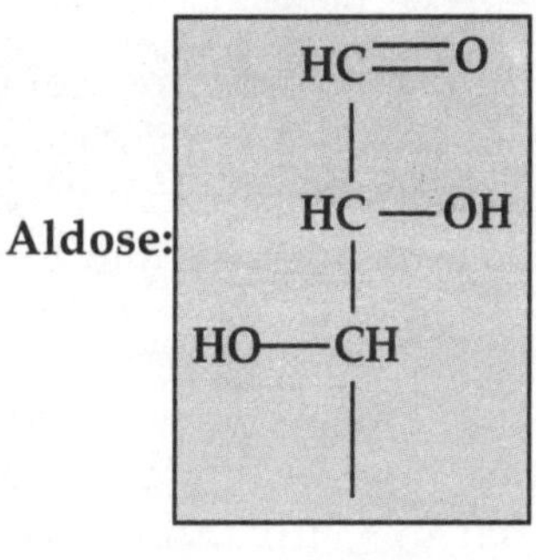

Acetal:

H, C, OR_1, OR_2

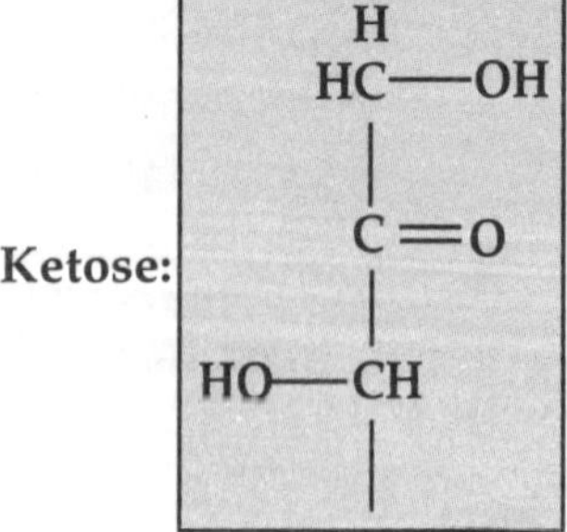

Hemiacetal:

H, C, OR_1, OH

A carbonyl can add water or alcohol to form a hemiacetal:

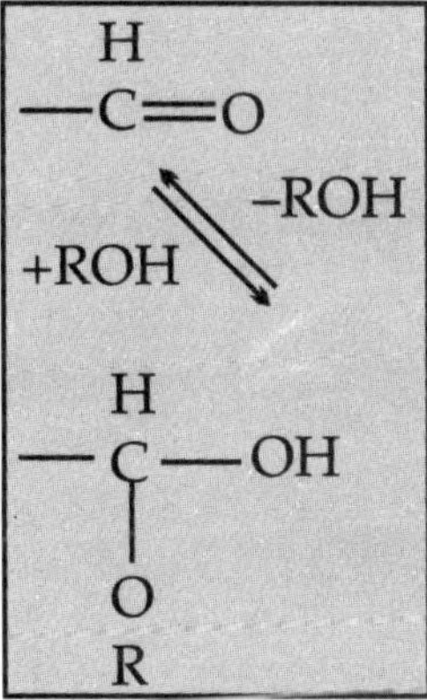

Fig. 11.1

The alcohol may be a portion of the carbohydrate molecule and thus, there can be ring formation. For most carbohydrates there exists an equilibrium between the aldehyde or keto form of the hemiacetal. Aldoses and ketoses cam be inter converted at either alkaline or acid pHs. Some near neutrality.

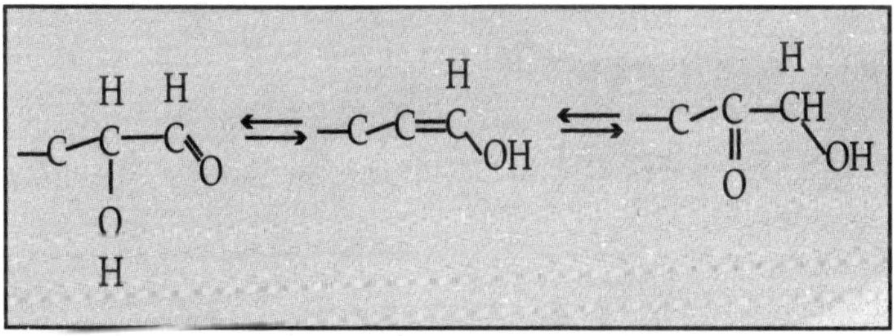

Fig. 11.2

Reactions of sugars Catalyzed Enolization by alkali Endiol formation

Lobry de Bruyn-Albreda van Eckenstein Reaction.

D-glucose
Enediol
D-mannose
C=O
C-OH
HO-C
HC-OH
HC-OH
CH2OH
C-OH
C-OH
HO-CH
HC-OH
HC-OH
CH2OH
C=
HO-CH
HO-CH
HC-OH
HC-OH
CH2OH
CH2OH
C=O
HO-CH
HC-OH
HC-OH
CH2OH
D-fructose

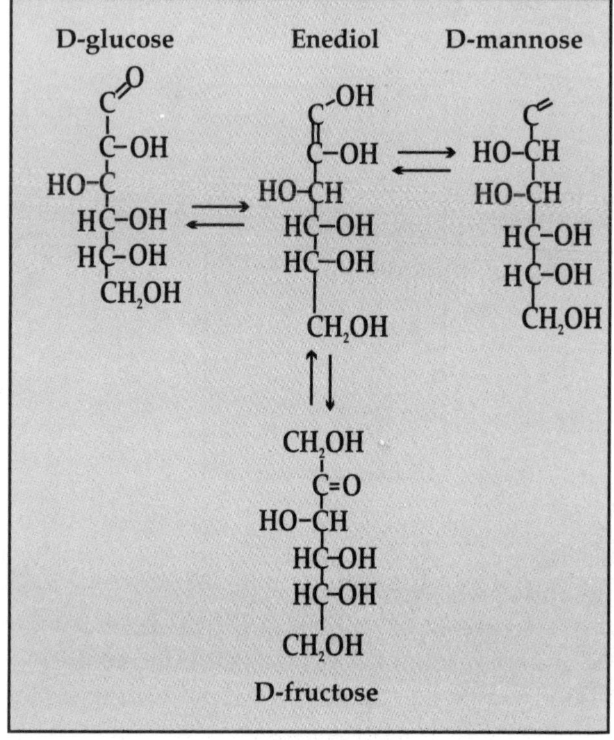

Fig. 11.3

Dehydration, thermal degredation

Osone formation

Final products may have intense colors, odors, off-flavours.

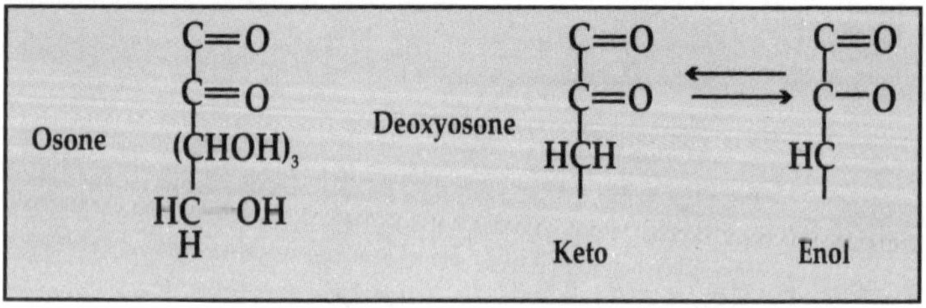

Osone
C=O
C=O
(CHOH)3
HC OH
H
Deoxyosone
C=O
C=O
HCH
C=O
C-O
HC
Keto
Enol

Fig. 11.4: **Osone**

Near neutrality, it is possible to convert an aldehyde to a deoxyosone as follows:

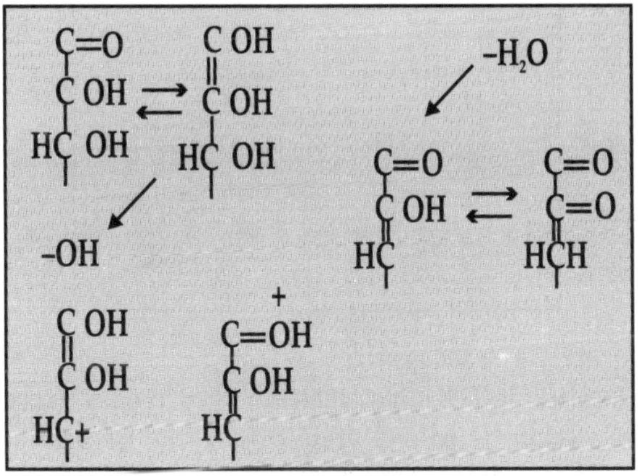

C=O
C OH
HC OH
C OH
C OH
HC OH
-OH
-H2O
C=O
C OH
HC
C=O
C=O
HCH
C OH
C OH
HC+
+
C=OH
C OH
HC

Fig. 11.5

The deoxyhexosone can be dehydrated by heating to yield more conjugated products:

HC=O
C—OH
HC
HC—OH
HC—OH
H—OH
OH
HC=O
C—OH
HC
HC+
HC—OH
HC—OH
H
HC=O
C—OH
+
HC
HC
HC—OH
HC—OH
H
HC=O
C=O
HC
HC
HC—OH
HC—OH
H
-H+

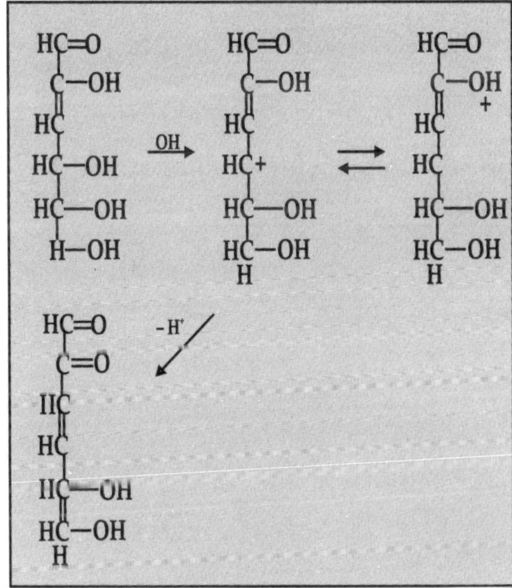

Fig. 11.6

In dilute alkali, two aldehydes can react as follows:

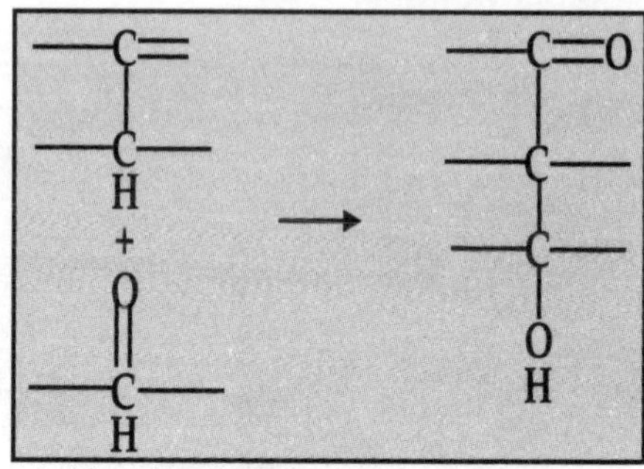

Fig. 11.7

In alkaline conditions, it is relatively easy to remove a proton that is alpha to a double bond. The resulting ion can undergo a keto-enol shift.

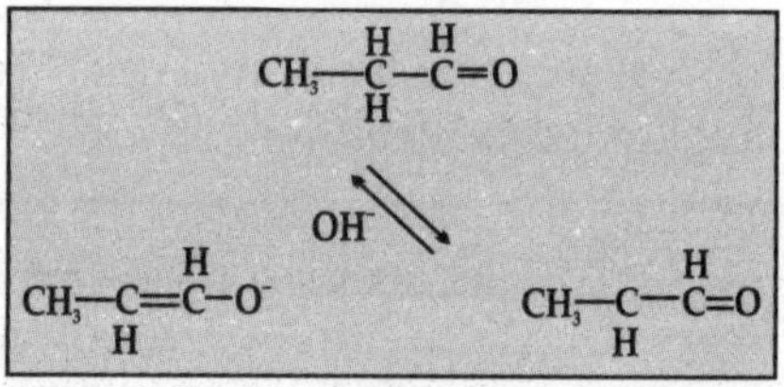

$$CH_3{-}CH_2{-}CH{=}O$$

$$CH_3{-}CH{=}CH{-}O^- \rightleftharpoons^{OH^-} CH_3{-}\overset{-}{C}H{-}CH{=}O$$

Fig. 11.8

This can now react with another aldehyde to form an addition product:

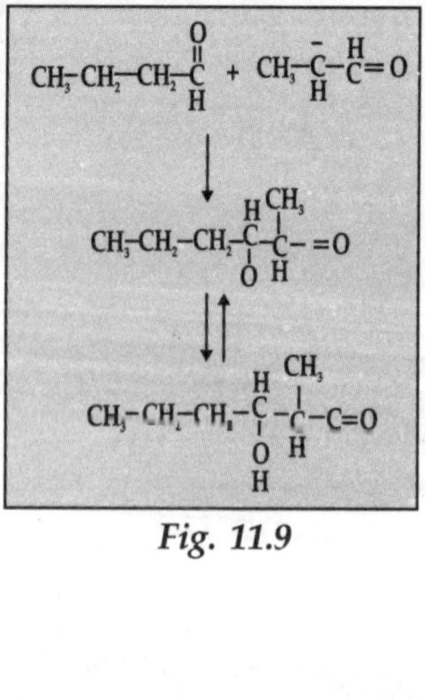

$$CH_3{-}CH_2{-}CH_2{-}CH{=}O + CH_3{-}\overset{-}{C}H{-}CH{=}O$$

$$\downarrow$$

$$CH_3{-}CH_2{-}CH_2{-}CH(O^-){-}CH(CH_3){-}CH{=}O$$

$$\rightleftharpoons$$

$$CH_3{-}CH_2{-}CH_2{-}CH(OH){-}CH(CH_3){-}CH{=}O$$

Fig. 11.9

The product contains and aldehyde and an alcohol and is know as an Aldol. The reaction is called an aldol condensation. Upon heating a molecule of water can be removed to yield:

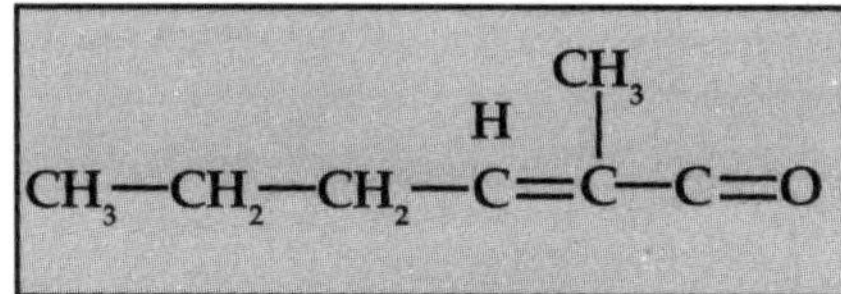

Fig. 11.10

Caramelization

Sucrose - 200° C

1. $2C_{12}H_{22}O_{11}$ = $4H_20$ $C_{24}H_{36}O_{18}$ Caramelan
2. $3C_{12}H_{22}O_{11}$ = $8H_20$ $C_{36}H_{50}O_{25}$ Caramelen
3. Continued heating yields humin or caramelin

   $C_{125}H_{188}O_{80}$

   Sucrose at 160° C

   Sucrose $\rightarrow$ Glucose + Fructose

Caramel Colours

Acid fast caramel

Glucose or sucrose + NH_4HSO_3

Ammonium bisulfate caramel

Cola beverages

Brewers caramel

Glucose or Sucrose

Ammonium bisulfite caramel + $NH4^+$

Beer, ale

Bakers Caramel

Glucose $\xrightarrow{\Delta}$ Brown polymers

Sucrose $\xrightarrow{\Delta}$ Brown polymers

Caramel colours contain:

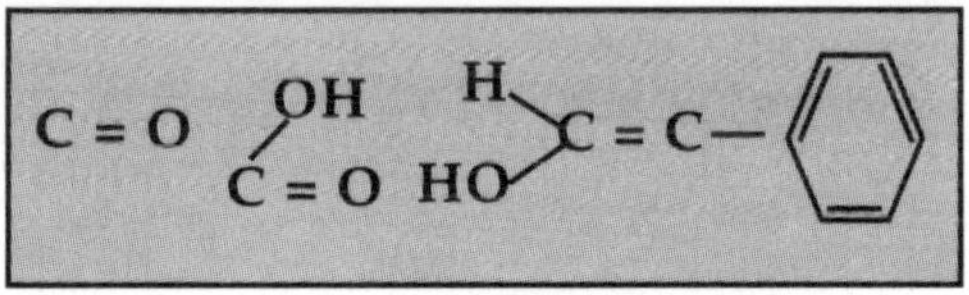

Fig. 11.11

Reaction rate increase as a function of increasing temperature and pH

Rate at pH 8.0 = 10 X rate at pH 5.8

Some Related Products:

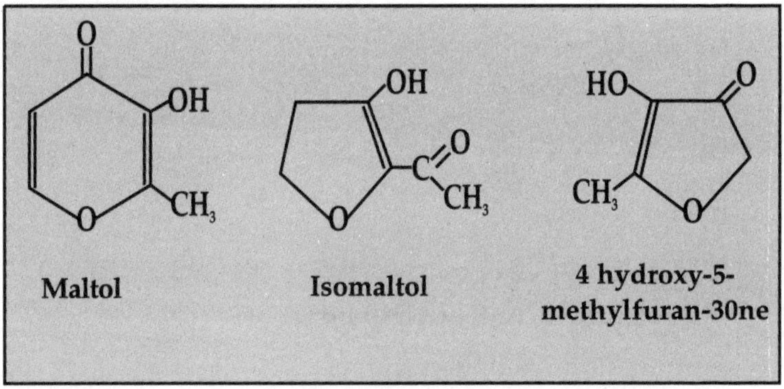

Fig. 11.12

12 Glycosylation

Glycosylation is the enzymatic process that links saccharides to produce glycans, either free or attached to proteins and lipids. This enzymatic process produces one of four fundamental components of all cells (along with nucleic acids, proteins, and lipids) and also provides a co-translational and post-translational modification mechanism that modulates the structure and function of membrane and secreted proteins. The majority of proteins synthesized in the rough ER undergo glycosylation. It is an enzyme-directed site-specific process, as opposed to the non-enzymatic chemical reaction of glycation. Glycosylation is also present in the cytoplasm and nucleus as the O-GlcNAc modification. Six classes of glycans are produced: *N*-linked glycans attached to the amide nitrogen of asparagine side chains, *O*-linked glycans attached to the hydroxy oxygen of serine and threonine side chains; glycosaminoglycans attached to the hydroxy oxygen of serine; glycolipids in which the glycans are attached to ceramide, hyaluronan which is unattached to either protein or lipid, and GPI anchors which link proteins to lipids through glycan linkages.

Purpose

The polysaccharide chains attached to the target proteins serve various functions. For instance, some proteins do not fold correctly unless they are glycosylated first. Also, polysaccharides linked at the amide nitrogen of asparagine in the protein confer stability on some secreted glycoproteins. Experiments have shown that glycosylation in this case is not a strict requirement for proper folding, but the unglycosylated protein degrades quickly. Glycosylation may play a role in cell-cell adhesion (a mechanism employed by cells of the immune system), as well.

Mechanisms

There are various mechanisms for glycosylation, although all share several common features:

- Glycosylation is an enzymatic process;
- The donor molecule is an activated nucleotide sugar;
- The process is site-specific.

Types of Glycosylation

N-linked Glycosylation

N-linked glycosylation is important for the folding of some eukaryotic proteins. The *N*-linked glycosylation process occurs in eukaryotes and widely in archaea, but very rarely in bacteria.

For *N*-linked oligosaccharides, a 14-sugar precursor is first added to the asparagine in the polypeptide chain of the target protein. The structure of this precursor is common to most eukaryotes, and contains 3 glucose, 9 mannose, and 2 *N*-acetylglucosamine molecules. A complex set of reactions attaches this branched chain to a carrier molecule called dolichol, and then it is transferred to the appropriate point on the polypeptide chain as it is translocated into the ER lumen.

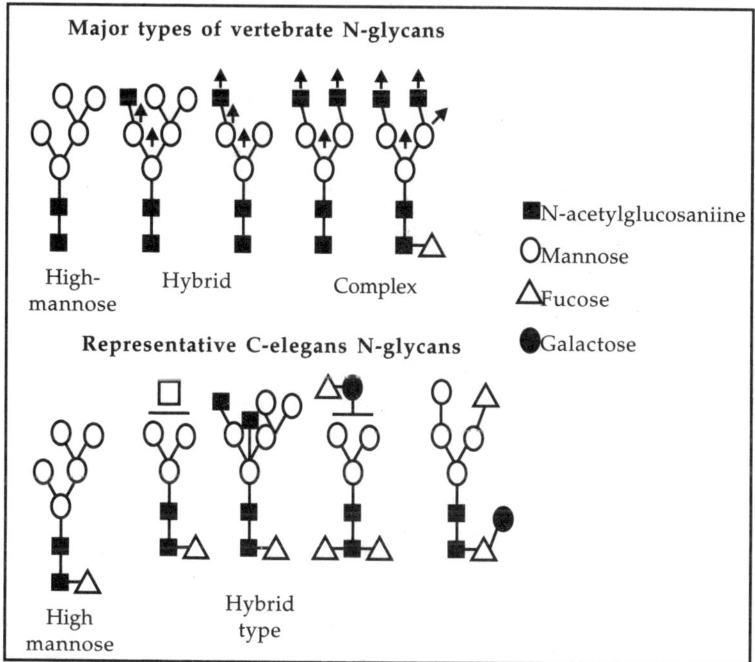

Fig 12.1: **Comparative overview of the major types of vertebrate N-glycan subtypes and some representative *C. elegans* N-glycans**

There are three major types of *N*-linked saccharides: high-mannose oligosaccharides, complex oligosaccharides and hybrid oligosaccharides.

- High-mannose is, in essence, just two *N*-acetylglucosamines with many mannose residues, often almost as many as are seen in the precursor oligosaccharides before it is attached to the protein.
- Complex oligosaccharides are so named because they can contain almost any number of the other types of saccharides, including more than the original two *N*-acetylglucosamines.

Proteins can be glycosylated by both types of oligos on different portions of the protein. Whether an oligosaccharide is high-mannose or complex is thought to depend on its accessibility to saccharide-modifying proteins in the Golgi. If the saccharide is relatively inaccessible, it will most likely stay in its original high-mannose form. If it is accessible, then it is likely that many of the mannose residues will be cleaved off and the saccharide will be further modified by the addition of other types of group as discussed above.

The oligosaccharide chain is attached by oligosaccharyl transferase to asparagine occurring in the tripeptide sequence Asn-X-Ser, Asn-X-Thr or Asn-X-Cys, where X could be any amino acid except Pro. This sequence is known as a glycosylation *sequon*. After attachment, once the protein is correctly folded, the three glucose residues are removed from the chain and the protein is available for export from the ER. The glycoprotein thus formed is then transported to the Golgi where removal of further mannose residues may take place. However, glycosylation itself does not seem to be as necessary for correct transport targeting of the protein, as one might think. Studies involving drugs that block certain steps in glycosylation, or mutant cells deficient in a glycosylation enzyme, still produce otherwise-structurally-normal proteins that are correctly targeted, and this interference does not seem to interfere severely with the viability of the cells. Mature glycoproteins may contain a variety of oligomannose *N*-linked oligosaccharides containing between 5 and 9 mannose residues. Further removal of mannose residues leads to a 'core' structure containing 3 mannose, and 2 *N*-acetylglucosamine residues, which may then be elongated with a variety of different monosaccharides including galactose, *N*-acetylglucosamine, *N*-acetylgalactosamine, fucose and sialic acid.

O-linked Glycosylation

O-N-acetylgalactosamine (O-GalNAc)

O-linked glycosylation occurs at a later stage during protein processing, probably in the Golgi apparatus. This is the addition of N-acetyl-galactosamine to serine or threonine residues by the enzyme *UDP-N-acetyl-D-galactosamine: polypeptide N-acetylgalactosaminyltransferase* (EC 2.4.1.41), followed by other carbohydrates (such as galactose and sialic acid). This process is important for certain types of proteins such as proteoglycans, which involves the addition of glycosaminoglycan chains to an initially unglycosylated "proteoglycan core protein." These additions are usually serine *O*-linked glycoproteins, which seem to have one of two main functions. One function involves secretion to form components of the extracellular matrix, adhering one cell to another by interactions between the large sugar complexes of proteoglycans. The other main function is to act as a component of mucosal secretions, and it is the high concentration of carbohydrates that tends to give mucus its "slimy" feel. Proteins that circulate in the blood are not normally *O*-glycosylated, with the exception of IgA1 and IgD (two types of antibody) and C1-inhibitor.

O-fucose

O-fucose is added between the second and third conserved cysteines of EGF-like repeats in the Notch protein, and other substrates by GDP-fucose protein *O*-fucosyltransferase 1, and to Thrombospondin repeats by GDP-fucose protein *O*-fucosyltransferase 2. In the case of EGF-like repeats, the *O*-fucose may be further elongated to a tetrasaccharide by sequential addition of N-acetylglucosamine (GlcNAc), galactose, and sialic acid, and for Thrombospondin repeats, may be elongated to a disaccharide by the addition of glucose. Both of these fucosyltransferases have been localized to the endoplasmic reticulum, which is unusual for glycosyltransferases, most of which function in the Golgi apparatus.

O-glucose

O-glucose is added between the first and second conserved cysteines of EGF-like repeats in the Notch protein, and possibly other substrates by an unidentified *O*-glucosyltransferase.

O-N-acetylglucosamine (O-GlcNAc)

O-GlcNAc is added to serines or threonines by *O*-GlcNAc transferase. *O*-GlcNAc appears to occur on serines and threonines that would otherwise be phosphorylated by serine/threonine kinases. Thus, if phosphorylation occurs, *O*-GlcNAc does not, and *vice versa*. This is an incredibly important finding because phosphorylation/dephosphorylation has become a scientific paradigm for the regulation of signaling within cells. A massive amount of cancer research is focused on phosphorylation. Ignoring the involvement of this form of glycosylation, which clearly appears to act in concert with phosphorylation, means that a lot of current research is missing at least half of the picture. *O*-GlcNAc addition and removal also appear to be key regulators of the pathways that are deregulated in diabetes mellitus. The gene encoding the *O*-GlcNAc removal enzyme has been linked to non-insulin dependent diabetes mellitus. It is the terminal step in a nutrient-sensing hexosamine signaling pathway.

GPI Anchor

A special form of glycosylation is the *GPI anchor*. This form of glycosylation functions to attach a protein to a hydrophobic lipid anchor, via a glycan chain.

C-mannosylation

A mannose sugar is added to tryptophan residues in Thrombospondin repeats. This is an unusual modification both because the sugar is linked to a carbon rather than a reactive atom like a nitrogen or oxygen and because the sugar is linked to a tryptophan residue rather than an asparagine or serine/threonine.

GLYCATION

Glycation (sometimes called non-enzymatic glycosylation) is the result of a sugar molecule, such as fructose or glucose, bonding to a protein or lipid molecule without the controlling action of an enzyme. All blood sugars are reducing molecules. Glycation may occur either inside the body (endogenous glycation) or outside the body (exogenous glycation). Enzyme-controlled addition of sugars to protein or lipid molecules is termed glycosylation; glycation is a haphazard process that impairs the functioning of biomolecules, whereas glycosylation occurs at defined sites on the target molecule and is required in order for the molecule to function. Much of the early laboratory research work on fructose glycations used inaccurate assay techniques that led to drastic underestimation of the importance of fructose in glycation

Exogenous

Exogenous, meaning *outside the body*, may also be referred to as *dietary* or *pre-formed*. Exogenous glycations and Advanced Glycation Endproducts (AGEs) are typically formed when sugars are cooked with proteins or fats. Temperatures over 120°C (~248°F) greatly accelerate the reactions, but lower temperatures with longer cooking times also promote their formation.

These compounds are absorbed by the body during digestion with about 30% efficiency. Browning reactions (usually Maillard type reactions) are evidence of pre-formed glycations. Indeed, sugar is often added to products such as french fries and baked goods to enhance browning. Glycation may also contribute to the formation of acrylamide a potential carcinogen, during cooking. Until recently, it was thought that exogenous glycations and AGEs were negligible contributors to inflammation and disease states, but recent work has shown that they are important Although most of the research work has been done with reference to diabetes, these results are most likely important for all people, as exogenous AGEs are implicated in the initiation of retinal dysfunction, cardiovascular diseases, type II diabetes, and many other age-related chronic diseases.

Food manufacturers have added AGEs to foods, especially in the last 50 years, as flavor enhancers and colorants to improve appearance Foods with significant browning, caramelization, or with directly added preformed AGEs can be exceptionally high in these proinflammatory and disease initiating compounds. A very partial listing of foods with very high exogenous AGEs includes: donuts, barbecued meats, cake, and dark colored soda pop.

Endogenous

Endogenous glycations occur mainly in the bloodstream to a small proportion of the absorbed simple sugars: glucose, fructose, and galactose. The balance of the sugar molecules is used for metabolic processes. It appears that fructose and galactose have approximately *ten times* the glycation activity of glucose, the primary body fuel. Glycation is the first step in the evolution of these molecules through a complex series of very slow reactions in the body known as Amadori reactions, Schiff base reactions, and Maillard reactions; all lead to advanced glycation endproducts (AGEs). Some AGEs are benign, but others are more reactive than the sugars they are derived from, and are implicated in many age-related chronic diseases such as: type I and II diabetes mellitus (beta cell damage), cardiovascular diseases (the endothelium, fibrinogen, and collagen are damaged), Alzheimer's disease (amyloid proteins are side-products of the reactions progressing to AGEs), cancer (acrylamide and other side-products are released), peripheral neuropathy (the myelin is attacked), and other sensory losses such as deafness (due to demyelination) and blindness (mostly due to microvascular damage in the retina). This range of diseases is the result of the very basic level at which glycations interfere with molecular and cellular functioning throughout the body and the release of highly-oxidizing side-products such as hydrogen peroxide.

Glycated substances are eliminated from the body slowly, since the renal clearance factor is only about 30%. This implies that the half-life of a glycation within the body is about double the average cell life. Red blood cells have a consistent lifespan of 120 days and are easily accessible for measurement of recent increased presence of glycating product. This fact is used in monitoring blood sugar control in diabetes by monitoring the glycated hemoglobin level, also known as HbA1c. As a consequence, long-lived cells (such as nerves, brain cells), long-lasting proteins (such as eye crystalline and collagen), and DNA may accumulate substantial damage over time. Metabolically-active cells such as the glomeruli in the kidneys, retina cells in the eyes, and beta cells (insulin-producing) in the pancreas are also at high risk of damage. The endothelial cells of the blood vessels are damaged directly by glycations, which are implicated in atherosclerosis, for example. Atherosclerotic plaque tends to accumulate at areas of high blood flow (such as the entrance to the coronary arteries) due to the increased presentation of sugar molecules, glycations and glycation end-products at these points. Damage by glycation results in stiffening of the collagen in the blood vessel walls, leading to high blood pressure. Glycations also cause weakening of the collagen in the blood vessel walls, which may lead to micro- or macro-aneurisms; this may cause strokes if in the brain.

ALAGEBRIUM

Alagebrium (formerly known as ALT-711) is a drug produced by Alteon Corporation, which is currently being evaluated in clinical trials. It is the first drug to be clinically tested for the purpose of breaking the crosslinks caused by advanced glycation endproducts (A.G.E.s), thereby reversing one of the main mechanisms of aging Through this effect Alagebrium is designed to reverse the stiffening of blood vessel walls that contributes to hypertension and cardiovascular disease, as well as many other forms of degradation associated with protein crosslinking.

A.G.E.s are permanent carbohydrate structures that form when carbohydrates bind to proteins, lipids and DNA.

Many proteins, including structural proteins such as collagen and elastin, play an integral role in the architecture of tissues and organs and maintenance of cardiovascular elasticity and vascular wall integrity. Diabetic individuals form excessive amounts of A.G.E.s earlier in life than non-diabetic individuals. This process can impair the normal function of organs that depend on flexibility for normal function, such as blood vessels and cardiac muscle. The formation of A.G.E. crosslinks leads to increased stiffness and loss of function of tissues and organs, and abnormal protein accumulation, which together cause many of the complications of aging and diabetes. A.G.E.s are also known to induce oxidative stress, in which reactive molecules provoke the underlying component of inflammation.

Pharmacologic intervention with alagebrium directly targets the biochemical pathway leading to the stiffness of the cardiovascular system. Removal of the A.G.E.s by cleavage of the abnormal crosslinking bonds has been associated with diminished inflammatory and sclerotic signaling pathways. These pathways are responsible for the deposition of abnormal amounts of matrix proteins that physically stiffen tissues. The presence of A.G.E. crosslinks also renders tissues and organs less susceptible to normal turnover thus enhancing the presence of these abnormal bonds on various molecules. Importantly, alagebrium does not disrupt the natural carbohydrate modification to proteins, intra-molecular crosslinking or peptide bonds that are responsible for maintaining the normal integrity of the collagen chain. Thus, normal structure and function is preserved while abnormal crosslinking is reduced.

The chemical compound had been discovered many years ago, and had traveled a circuitous route through academia, research firms, and finally, Alteon. There are two prominent attributes to Alagebrium (as Alteon renamed it). The first is that it is not a difficult compound to synthesize.

An active black market rose very quickly after the early Phase I and II tests came in. Independent, lab-tested, certified for purity product was available for a short time on the grey market at about $3 per gram.

Although Alagebrium has shown very promising Phase I and II clinical trials, active research stopped because Alteon had run out of operating cash Alteon, having a huge amount of convertible preferred stock hanging over its head (held by Genentech), had increasing difficulty raising subsequent levels of venture capital until finally, it was unavailable at any price. On 25 July, 2007 Alteon was essentially bought for its corporate shell by a three-man operation developing another medication that needed a corporate shell in order to move fast. The company changed its name to Synvista Therapeutics, Inc. now with perhaps three employees in the United States, and outsources its research, (probably none of it on Alagebrium, despite the website's assertions).

One conclusion that could easily be derived from the published research is that Alagebrium works first and fastest on those areas with the most blood-to-surface coverage and that are constantly in a state of higher levels of hemodynamic pressure, such as the large and small chambers of the heart, as well as the atriums, and potentially, the valves. Because testing for regulatory approval looks for quick answers for severe problems in order to meet the 'need' hurdles of the FDA, and given the impatience of the venture capital markets, Alteon never engaged in long-term tests seeking FDA approval of the medication for conditions other than heart treatment, so the patent applied for was a 'use' patent for just that. Given the relationship between surface-area coverage under pressure and short-terms results, testing for conditions such as diabetic neuropathy, or long-term low-dose prohylactic use for aging hearts, which would have taken years, was never an option for Alteon. Although the medication had dramatic positive results in the tests for efficacy, the molecule is not difficult to replicate, which is a negative vis-a-vis obtaining approval and satisfying investors that they are buying into an exclusively-owned product. So a lack of patent protection, and ease of replication by others, obviously made the venture investment community lose faith before an approved product arrived.

13 Glycomics

Glycomics, an analogous term to genomics and proteomics, is the comprehensive study of glycomes (the entire complement of sugars, whether free or present in more complex molecules, of an organism), including genetic, physiologic, pathologic, and other aspects Glycomics "is the systematic study of all glycan structures of a given cell type or organism" and is a subset of glycobiology The term glycomics is derived from the chemical prefix for sweetness or a sugar, "glyco-", and was formed to follow the naming convention established by genomics (which deals with genes) and proteomics (which deals with proteins).

Challenges

- The complexity of sugars: regarding their structures, they are not linear instead they are highly branched. Moreover, glycans can be modified (modified sugars), this increase its complexity.
- Complex biosynthetic pathways for gylcans.

- Usually glycans are found either bound to protein (glycoprotein) or conjugated with lipids (glycolipids).
- Unlike genomes, glycans are highly dynamic.

This area of research has to deal with an inherent level of complexity not seen in other areas of applied biology. 68 building blocks (molecules for DNA, RNA and proteins; categories for lipids; types of sugar linkages for saccharides) provide the structural basis for the molecular choreography that constitutes the entire life of a cell. DNA and RNA have four building blocks each (the nucleosides or nucleotides). Lipids are divided into eight categories based on ketoacyl and isoprene. Proteins have 20 (the amino acids). Saccharides have 32 types of sugar linkages. While these building blocks can be attached only linearly for proteins and genes, they can be arranged in a branched array for saccharides, further increasing the degree of complexity.

Importance

To answer of this question one should know the different and important functions of glycans. The following are some of those functions:

- Gylcoproteins found on the cell surface play a critical role in bacterial and viral recognition.
- They are involved in cellular signaling pathways.
- They affect the stability and folding of proteins.
- There are many glycan-specific diseases.

Tools Used

The following are examples of the commonly used techniques in glycan analysis.

High Resolution Mass Spectrometry

The most applied method in which the glycan part of a glycoprotein is separated from the protein and subjected to analysis by multiple rounds of mass spectrometry. In case of glycolipids, they can be analyzed directly without separation of the lipid component. Mass spectrometry can be used in conjunction with HPLC.

Table 13.1: Advantages and disadvantages of mass spectrometry in glycan analysis

Advantages	Disadvantages
Applicable for small sample size.	Destructive method.
Useful if the sample contain multiple glycan of any type.	No information about the modified glycan (e.g. sulfation and acetylation).
For glycoprotein, can identify the site of attachment between the glycan and the protein	Need separate experimental design for every glycan subtype.

Lectin and Antibody Array

It provides high-throughput screening of many samples containing glycans. This method use either naturally occurring lectins or artificial monoclonal antibodies, where both are immobilized on a certain chip and incubated with a fluorescent glycoprotein sample.

Metabolic labeling of glycans can be used as a way to detect glycan structures. A well known strategy involves the use of azide-labeled sugars which can be reacted using the Staudinger ligation. This method has been used for in vitro and in vivo imaging of glycans.

OMICS

The English-language neologism omics informally refers to a field of study in biology ending in the suffix *-omics,* such as genomics or proteomics. The related neologism omes addresses the objects of study of such fields, such as the genome or proteome respectively. Users of the suffix *"-om-"* frequently take it as referring to *totality* of some sort.

Origin

Because of the success of large-scale genome sequencing, the suffix "*-om-*" has been picked up by a wide array of other large-scale quantitative biology fields.

Early Adopters of "omes"

Bioinformaticians and molecular biologists figured amongst the first scientists to start to apply the "-ome" suffix widely. Some early advocates were bioinformaticians in Cambridge, UK, where there were many early bioinformatics labs such as the MRC centre, Sanger centre, and EBI (European Bioinformatics Institute). For example, the MRC centre is where the first genome and proteome projects were carried out.

Acceptance

Many "omes" beyond the original "genome" have become useful and have been widely adopted by research scientists. "Proteomics" has become well-established as a term for studying proteins at a large scale. "Omes" can provide an easy short-hand to encapsulate a field; for example, an interactomics study is clearly recognisable as relating to large-scale analyses of gene-gene, protein-protein, or protein-ligand interactions. Researchers are rapidly taking up omes and omics, as shown by the explosion of the use of these terms in PubMed since the mid '90s.

Established "omes"

- The *transcriptome*, the mRNA complement of an entire organism, tissue type, or cell; with its associated field *transcriptomics*.
- The *proteome*, the protein complement of an entire organism, tissue type, or cell; with its associated field *proteomics*.
- The *metabolome*, the totality of metabolites in an organism; with its associated field *metabolomics*.

- The *metallome*, the totality of metal and metalloid species; with its associated field *metallomics*.
- The *lipidome*, the totality of lipids; with its associated field *lipidomics*.
- The *glycome*, the totality of glycans, carbohydrate structures of an organism, a cell or tissue type; with its associated field *glycomics*.
- The *interactome*, the totality of the molecular interactions in an organism *a once proposed field of interactomics* has generally become known as systems biology.
- The *spliceome* spliceosome), the totality of the alternative splicing protein isoforms; with its associated field *spliceomics*.
- The *Orfeome* refers to the totality of DNA sequences that begin with the initiation codon ATG, nd with a nonsense codon, and contain no stop codon. uch sequences may therefore encode part or all of a protein.
- The *speechome*. (BBC article on the Speechome Project)
- The *mechanome* refers to the force and mechanical systems at work within an organism.
- The *phenome* - the organism itself. The phenome is to the phenotype what the genome is to the gene. The phenome can also be the complete list of phenotypic mutants available for a species.
- The *exposome* - the collection of an individual's environmental exposures.

Newer "omics" and "omes"

- *Ubiquitome*: The complement of ubiquitin conjugated proteins within the proteome.
- *Receptorome*: The portion of the genome encoding receptors.
- *Kinome*: The totality of protein kinases in a cell.

- *Kinomics*: The study of the kinome.
- *Physiome*: Related to physiology.
- *Physiomics*: The associated field of study.
- *Neurome*: The complete neural makeup of an organism. A word which a neurobiologist might utter in the future.
- *Neuromics*: The study of the neurome.

  Note: Neurome and Neuromics are now the names of Biotech companies. The term 'Neurome' which is an attempt to develop an approach to catalog the Neurome.
- *Cytome*: The cellular composition of a tissue. This term is associated to cell sorting techniques.
- *Predictome*: A complete set of predictions.
- *Reactome*: A knowledge base of biological processes.
- *Connectome*: The connections between neurons. A Technicolour Approach to the Connectome (Nature)
- *Translatomics:* Analysis of actively transcribed mRNA molecules.
- *Transferome:* The complete set of genes within a genome that were acquired through horizontal gene transfer.

Unrelated *-omics*

The word "comic" does not use the "omics" suffix; it derives from Greek µ -" (*merriment*) + (an adjectival suffix), rather than presenting a truncation of "s?µ(at)-".

Similarly, the word "economy" is assembled from Greek " " (*household*) + µ " (*law* or *custom*), and "economic(s)" from " + " µ -" + ". The suffix -omics is sometimes used to create portmanteau words to refer to schools of economics such as Reaganomics.

PROTEOMICS

Proteomics is the large-scale study of proteins, particularly their structures and functions. Proteins are vital parts of living organisms, as they are the main components of the physiological metabolic pathways of cells. The term "proteomics" was first coined in 1997 to make an analogy with genomics, the study of the genes. The word "proteome" is a blend of "protein" and "genome", and was coined by Prof Marc Wilkins in 1994 while working on the concept as a PhD student The proteome is the entire complement of proteins, including the modifications made to a particular set of proteins, produced by an organism or system. This will vary with time and distinct requirements, or stresses, that a cell or organism undergoes.

Complexity of the Problem

After genomics, proteomics is often considered the next step in the study of biological systems. It is much more complicated than genomics mostly because while an organism's genome is more or less constant, the proteome differs from cell to cell and from time to time. This is because distinct genes are expressed in distinct cell types. This means that even the basic set of proteins which are produced in a cell needs to be determined.

In the past this was done by mRNA analysis, but this was found not to correlate with protein content It is now known that mRNA is not always translated into protein and the amount of protein produced for a given amount of mRNA depends on the gene it is transcribed from and on the current physiological state of the cell. Proteomics confirms the presence of the protein and provides a direct measure of the quantity present.

Examples of Post-translational Modifications

Phosphorylation

More importantly though, any particular protein may go through a wide variety of alterations which will have critical effects to its function. For example during cell signaling many enzymes and structural proteins can undergo phosphorylation. The addition of a phosphate to particular amino acids—most commonly serine and threonine mediated by serine/threonine kinases, or more rarely tyrosine mediated by tyrosine kinases—causes a protein to become a target for binding or interacting with a distinct set of other proteins that recognize the phosphorylated domain.

Because protein phosphorylation is one of the most-studied protein modifications many "proteomic" efforts are geared to determining the set of phosphorylated proteins in a particular cell or tissue-type under particular circumstances. This alerts the scientist to the signaling pathways that may be active in that instance.

Ubiquitination

Ubiquitin is a small protein that can be affixed to certain protein substrates by enzymes called E3 ubiquitin ligases. Determining which proteins are poly-ubiquitinated can be helpful in understanding how protein pathways are regulated. This is therefore an additional legitimate "proteomic" study. Similarly, once it is determined what substrates are ubiquitinated by each ligase, determining the set of ligases expressed in a particular cell type will be helpful.

Additional Modifications

Listing all the protein modifications that might be studied in a "Proteomics" project would require a discussion of most of biochemistry; therefore, a short list will serve here to illustrate the complexity of the problem. In addition to phosphorylation and ubiquitination, proteins can be subjected to methylation, acetylation, glycosylation, oxidation, nitrosylation, etc. Some proteins undergo ALL of these modifications, which nicely illustrates the potential complexity one has to deal with when studying protein structure and function.

Distinct Proteins are made under Distinct Settings

Even if one is studying a particular cell type, that cell may make different sets of proteins at different times, or under different conditions. Furthermore, as mentioned, any one protein can undergo a wide range of post-translational modifications.

Therefore a "proteomics" study can become quite complex very quickly, even if the object of the study is very restricted. In more ambitious settings, such as when a biomarker for a tumor is sought - when the proteomics scientist is obliged to study sera samples from multiple cancer patients - the amount of complexity that must be dealt with is as great as in any modern biological project.

Rationale for Proteomics

The key requirement in understanding protein function is to learn to correlate the vast array of potential protein modifications to particular phenotypic settings, and then determine if a particular post-translational modification is required for a function to occur.

Limitations to Genomic Study

Scientists are very interested in proteomics because it gives a much better understanding of an organism than genomics. First, the level of transcription of a gene gives only a rough estimate of its level of expression into a protein. An mRNA produced in abundance may be degraded rapidly or translated inefficiently, resulting in a small amount of protein. Second, as mentioned above many proteins experience post-translational modifications that profoundly affect their activities; for example some proteins are not active until they become phosphorylated. Methods such as phosphoproteomics and glycoproteomics are used to study post-translational modifications. Third, many transcripts give rise to more than one protein, through alternative splicing or alternative post-translational modifications. Fourth, many proteins form complexes with other proteins or RNA molecules, and only function in the presence of these other molecules. Finally, protein degradation rate plays an important role in protein content.

Methods of Studying Proteins

Determining Proteins which are Post-translationally Modified

One way in which a particular protein can be studied is to develop an antibody which is specific to that modification. For example, there are antibodies which only recognize certain proteins when they are tyrosine-phosphorylated; also, there are antibodies specific to other modifications. These can be used to determine the set of proteins that have undergone the modification of interest.

For sugar modifications, such as glycosylation of proteins, certain lectins have been discovered which bind sugars. These too can be used.

A more common way to determine post-translational modification of interest is to subject a complex mixture of proteins to electrophoresis in "two-dimensions", which simply means that the proteins are electrophoresed first in one direction, and then in another ... this allows small differences in a protein to be visualized by separating a modified protein from its unmodified form. This methodology is known as "two-dimensional gel electrophoresis".

Another approach has been developed called *Protomap* which combines *SDS-PAGE* with shotgun proteomics to enable detection of changes in gel-migration such as those caused by proteolysis or post translational modification.

Determining the Existence of Proteins in Complex Mixtures

Classically, antibodies to particular proteins or to their modified forms have been used in biochemistry and cell biology studies. These are among the most common tools used by practicing biologists today.

For more quantitative determinations of protein amounts, techniques such as ELISAs can be used.

For proteomic study, more recent techniques such as Matrix-assisted laser desorption/ionization have been employed for rapid determination of proteins in particular mixtures.

Establishing Protein-protein Interactions

Most proteins function in collaboration with other proteins, and one goal of proteomics is to identify which proteins interact. This is especially useful in determining potential partners in cell signaling cascades.

Several methods are available to probe protein-protein interactions. The traditional method is yeast two-hybrid analysis. New methods include protein microarrays, immunoaffinity chromatography followed by mass spectrometry, and experimental methods such as phage display and computational methods.

Practical Applications of Proteomics

One of the most promising developments to come from the study of human genes and proteins has been the identification of potential new drugs for the treatment of disease. This relies on genome and proteome information to identify proteins associated with a disease, which computer software can then use as targets for new drugs. For example, if a certain protein is implicated in a disease, its 3D structure provides the information to design drugs to interfere with the action of the protein. A molecule that fits the active site of an enzyme, but cannot be released by the enzyme, will inactivate the enzyme. This is the basis of new drug-discovery tools, which aim to find new drugs to inactivate proteins involved in disease. As genetic differences among individuals are found, researchers expect to use these techniques to develop personalized drugs that are more effective for the individual.

A computer technique which attempts to fit millions of small molecules to the three-dimensional structure of a protein is called "virtual ligand screening". The computer rates the quality of the fit to various sites in the protein, with the goal of either enhancing or disabling the function of the protein, depending on its function in the cell. A good example of this is the identification of new drugs to target and inactivate the HIV-1 protease. The HIV-1 protease is an enzyme that cleaves a very large HIV protein into smaller, functional proteins. The virus cannot survive without this enzyme; therefore, it is one of the most effective protein targets for killing HIV.

Biomarkers

Understanding the proteome, the structure and function of each protein and the complexities of protein-protein interactions will be critical for developing the most effective diagnostic techniques and disease treatments in the future.

An interesting use of proteomics is using specific protein biomarkers to diagnose disease. A number of techniques allow to test for proteins produced during a particular disease, which helps to diagnose the disease quickly. Techniques include western blot, immunohistochemical staining, enzyme linked immunosorbent assay (ELISA) or mass spectrometry. The following are some of the diseases that have characteristic biomarkers that physicians can use for diagnosis.

Alzheimer's Disease

In Alzheimer's disease, elevations in beta secretase create amyloid/beta-protein, which causes plaque to build up in the patient's brain, which is thought to play a role in dementia. Targeting this enzyme decreases the amyloid/beta-protein and so slows the progression of the disease. A procedure to test for the increase in amyloid/beta-protein is immunohistochemical staining, in which antibodies bind to specific antigens or biological tissue of amyloid/beta-protein.

Heart Disease

Heart disease is commonly assessed using several key protein based biomarkers. Standard protein biomarkers for CVD include interleukin-6, interleukin-8, serum amyloid A protein, fibrinogen, and troponins. (cTnI) cardiac troponin I increases in concentration within 3 to 12 hours of initial cardiac injury and can be found elevated days after an acute myocardial infarction. A number of commercial antibody based assays as well as other methods are used in hospitals as primary tests for acute heart infractions.

Index

P

R

S

T